The Traveler's Confessional

by

J. Levi

Printed in the United States of America
First Paperback Edition 2018

First Paperback Edition | ISBN 978-0-9997354-0-4
Library of Congress Control Number: 2018904437

Published by: J. Levi Brown
Copyright © J. Levi Brown | 2018
1-6024844181 | 1-6449800421 | TXu 2-092-182

Cover: Detail of Street Mural
Santiago, Chile | Artist Unknown
Design and Digital Edits by JLB

TheTravelersConfessional@gmail.com

Dedication

For my father's history and my mother within,

to those whose dreams come true.

To yours and mine, the influence refined,

so perfect yet askew.

For my daughter, Iliani Serene –

may you always find your path.

Contents

Prologue

I have finally arrived at Valhalla, or whatever the Incas call it, but everyone is leaving. I will be a part of the next wave. All my friends have been here for days, but I spent too much time in Cuenca and missed the party.

Their bags are packed and hiding under the hammock and café tables. I set my pack down next to theirs and exchange stories, until eventually the conversation turns into goodbyes. They walk into town and catch their bus, leaving me to join a new tribe in the Valley of Longevity.

I've only just met Paul, Myra, and Mateo, but we all are on the same mission. We wander the hillside, cross the river, and look for animals and other natural beauties, but our only true interest is in finding the San Pedro mescaline cactus.

Some guy named Pico prepares this mixture for the travelers to the area. He has a comfortable setting and knows how to do this right. Unfortunately for us, Pico was arrested two weeks ago.

For the last two nights, we've collected cactus stalks and blended them into horrific smoothies. The effects have not been as advertised. Instead, they've just tasted like prickly mud shakes with no reward for enduring the taste. We're on our own until the universe sends some help. Fortunately for us, that will only be a few hours from now.

On the third day, we leave the hostel to collect more stalks again. We stop in the town center and are sitting against the stone fountain when Amanda passes by.

We met Amanda last night at the market. She is five years older than the rest of us, clothed in torn jeans and an alpaca shawl. Her dirty blonde hair blends into the shawl's patterns.

Amanda is the link between the local and the traveler. She bridges these two worlds. She is Canadian, but she's been in Ecuador for years, making her nearly native. We are lucky to have met her yesterday, but we are even more fortunate to see her just now, coming through the town square, while we sit with our skins in our bags not sure what to do next.

Amanda sees our stalks.

"Do you guys know what you're doing?"

"Not really," we all shamelessly nod and agree.

"Follow me."

Amanda leads us out of the town square, in the opposite direction of our lodging. We hike along a dirt road between the hills, until the town fades away behind us. Fallen trees line the dirt pathway down a slight slope, past a fire pit, to the wooden porch of the rustic two-story cabin. The walls are unpainted lumber, caked with dried mud. Amanda's house blends well with the old growth forest, seemingly made from these same materials, perhaps built when it was just a young forest.

Propped on the side of the house is a harvest of stalks. The kitchen looks like an afterthought, as an addition to the ground floor, which doesn't seem to blend in with the rest of the house. There is a propane camp stove on the table, robust enough to boil cactus skins for half a day to create the psychedelic concentrate.

Inside the cabin, the interior is barren and dusty. Lanterns illuminate the dark corners and cast shadows across the wooden floors. The wide balcony on the second floor underscores the large barn windows, none of which have glass. Overlooking the jungle's edge, my mind wanders into the Amazon basin below.

Fireflies flicker in the starry night sky, obscuring the boundaries between earth and her heavens. They trace the skies like little comets coming to rest in the grass, like tiny pixies fleeing heaven. Dara shows us one he caught, then releases it back into the wild.

The man in the moon has eyelashes and he winks at us, as he peaks over the horizon and shows us the rest of his face. Instantly, all the fireflies disappear into the bushes and turn off their butt-lights. They go away for the night as if father moon has just ushered them all to bed.

The Earth spins steadily under our feet. This is an earth induced spiritual retreat. All the questions of the universe are evident, we know how they are all connected, we are part of that ribbon.

Amanda hands us the keys to heaven and we all step through the doorway, as prophesized by the ancient Incas. Everything is perfectly aligned in a vortex of colors - the crowd, the house, the rhythm, the sunset, the forest, the hammock, the food, and of course, the fire.

There are ten of us, each acting as a link in a cohesive chain, each breathing the energy around us, sharing in the divine appreciation of the high Andes, and the valley view to the jungle floor. We give praise to Pachamama, our Mother Earth, and revel in the forest around us.

We are like-minded and pulsing these minds in rhythm with all creation. The campfire flames lick at the sky, like an upside-down waterfall, flowing endlessly into the starry ocean, creating the galaxies themselves. Our souls join to form our chain, forged in firelight, by the San Pedro cactus reign. Everything pulses in unison.

Time moves around us. The rules of reality are being rewritten and chaos of thought is inevitable. The sun is our majesty and it's reigning hot. The music, it's yellow and blue. Our campfire songs take physical form and walk around the logs, tapping each of us on the soul.

The trees have faces and the wind's wings brush across our shoulders. Paul and I look out from the balcony at all the Christmas lights. There are none, but we both see them. We are sharing visions while viewing the energy of the forest. Tiny crimson lights circle each of the branches, spiraling down the trunks before they disappear through their roots and into the earth.

I leave Paul on the balcony and wander alone to the frog pond behind the cabin. A tiny mud bank and a small grassy area flank the water, but this trip is about the trees. They are the universe's grand sentries, and they smile at me through the faces in their leaves. Their arms outstretch to form a net of protection, guarding me from bad spirits.

I sit at the base of the largest tree and sink into the mud. Leafy limbs reach down and snuggle me in their embrace, helping to hide me from the world. I am connected, I am invisible, I am entranced, I am one.

I close my eyes and curl into a ball. I am reborn and reflect upon the evolutions that have delivered me to heaven's doorway. I flashback to my youth, to the past that brought me tears, to the steps that brought me here, to my search for the truth.

Home Base Camp

1

T he smell of pine and campfires permeate my dreams.
I feel the cold, Alaskan waters in my bones. Nature
kisses my face and the ruggedness soaks my clothes. In
my sober waking moments, these sensations are usually
much closer to fish guts and sea water than the visions
that sustain my dreams.

The people here are rough around the edges. It
might scare me if they were in the city, but we are in their
home now. They welcome us. The mountains tower above,
guarding our passage. The glaciers serve as the remnants
of enemies who fought the northern chill and lost, only to
now sit frozen in time. My heart leaps and my soul giggles,
even though the mushrooms have finally worn off.

We share that, Colin and me, we seek to escape. Although we live within the same circles, we only grew close this last summer when I came back from Alaska the first time. We both dance close to the edges and never let the party stop. That is our nature and our bond.

Colin has natty dreadlocks and a drunken spirit. He is the wild one, the type that my cop parents warned me about. He smokes constantly, either cigarettes or his perfectly rolled joints.

Colin disappeared immediately after landing at the Anchorage airport. I quickly found him outside smoking, and thankfully, closer inspection revealed that he is only smoking tobacco. I walked up and lit my cigarette, and together we outlined the route to our summer home.

Last year, Amber and Stefan picked me up at baggage claim. This time is different. No one is here to greet us, we don't have a free ride and we don't have money for a taxi. Colin finds us a bus to the outskirts of town. We get out and hitch hike through the dawn and into lunchtime.

The conversations in these stranger's cars are familiar from last year, but they are still a welcome jolt. "Where ya from? You lookin' ta fish?"

When I was last on this highway, heading south for the fishing season, I had these very same conversations with other Alaskans. They love to talk about the many grandeurs of this state. I have also grown to love Alaska, these are shared sentiments that augment our excitement.

"People in Alaska are less hindered than those down south. The same struggles for success do not apply."

Colin engages our various drivers in philosophical debate while I stare out the window and analyze my fate.

When we arrive in Kenai, we immediately set up our campsites at the familiar Pacific Star campground that I know from last year. This little patch of forest beckoned me from 2,500 miles away. I am away from home, but I am home again. What type of people will we meet this summer, what will the days bring, and how smoothly will the days blend into the night? Oh, and where are the fish?

For two years now, I have been too eager to get here. The summer fishing season is not ready for us yet. There's still a winter chill in the air, and we are the first ones to arrive at the campground. I still half expect to see Ed and Jaybird camping around our old familiar fire pit, but I suppose they found other things to do over the last seven months.

They are not around, nor is anyone else. We are the only ones here. There is no welcoming party. There are no magical gates of Shangri La that open to receive us. Colin seems perfectly content with this, as I was when I first saw this patch of green last year.

"This is where I camped at the beginning of last summer. Ed was over there, and Jaybird was under that tree. I was hoping they'd be here, you would like them." I explain to Colin like a real-estate agent selling a house. Even though I will likely never see them again, I make sure to leave their patches undisturbed. I don't want to break some unwritten rule if they show up and find me camping on their dirt.

Colin is settling on my spot from last year, but I quickly claim it first. The trail is faded and overgrown, but I imagine the paths will gain distinction in a few weeks when the other transients influx into the area. The forest is deserted, but still, we remain calm.

We pitch our tents, grab our day packs, and swiftly begin to explore our borders and our boundaries. We leave our worldly possessions obscured by trees and walk out to the highway. After waiting ten minutes with our thumbs out, we jump into a small truck.

I never went this direction last year, the universe had other plans when it sent me Unko. We find an entirely new world just by driving in the other direction! This life lesson will eventually translate into boundless footprints, across multiple continents, but that's later.

Colin and I find campsites and canneries littered all throughout the forests, their inhabitants beaming with life and enthusiasm. We immediately move away from our isolated patch on the side of the highway and join the party at Dragnet's tent-town.

The air is chilly, but the atmosphere is electric. It is a congregation of kindred spirits. It reminds me of the parking lot at The Grateful Dead show, with intense and surreal environs which congeal into a social antithesis.

I see the office door, but I don't go there. Once someone opens it, I will need to integrate back to the socio-economic grid and get back to work. Instead, I join Colin who is already playing hacky-sack with a beer in his hand and his shirt in the dirt.

Most of us are first-time fish hippies, or as I prefer, *hip fishies*. We don't know if we need the silver run, the reds, chums, or humpies. We're talking salmon, right? When is the halibut run? We don't know, we're just having fun. The cannery has only just begun to harvest the roe, which means the fish are slow to start this year, but the ocean will soon open her mouth and expel fish for Dragnet and the other processing plants on the Kenai Peninsula.

Just a short hike away, on the rocky beaches of The Cook Inlet, we burn driftwood and return the essence to the universe in the form of smoke and flame. We find ways to pass the time, we don't need the fish.

This place is more than just a campsite. It is a commune, a hospice, a kibbutz. It is our safe house and we look out for each other. It has been three weeks and we are living pure, free from the grid, with nothing but time. This is cheap living out here in the bush, but it still isn't free. We all support each other. I haven't felt like I was part of a group collective like this since my tour in the Marine Corps. I never found peace in the service, but my peace found me when I found purpose.

Colin is the social honeybee who struts around with his stinger out. He is opportunistic but deceptively useful. He always starts the campfires at my barn parties in Walla Walla, and that tradition translates well here in Alaska. He cooks the meals, too! Kind of. We usually just take tin foil, fill it with noodles, potatoes, mushroom soup, and whatever else we can find into a little ball. Throw it into the fire and see how it comes out. The Hobo Stew.

When we want to treat ourselves to a nice dinner, we visit the Kasilof Bar for roadkill moose tacos. They're two for a dollar. We have a communal can of tobacco and some papers for smoking. That one guy with the clean shirt buys kegs of beer and keeps the tap open for all of us. We spend a lot of time at clean-shirt's camp, but within these endlessly long days and lack of duties, there is time to flourish in each of these micro-worlds that link throughout the forest.

The perpetual spring weather and sunny days put everyone in good spirits. We work on our home projects, improving our living environments. We play hours of hacky-sack and extend our spirits into our surroundings.

We are free to do as we please. The few people who work at the cannery always come back to camp smelling like fish and shampoo, since they have the luxury of the cannery showers. The rest of us must sneak in on Sundays if we wish to focus on hygiene.

For the first month, we hitchhike a few hundred miles in any given direction from our base camp at Dragnet forest. It is easy for us to pack our tents, walk fifty feet to the highway and hike to the next town for bluegrass festivals and green grass herbs. We don't have schedules.

A few hours south, in Homer, fate and fortune intertwine, blending my new world with my old one. In a freak chance of luck, Colin and I see some friends from our hometown, Durgan and Lyle! They are core to our crew and true to our roots.

Our oblivion is on full display to the fact that none of us knew the other was in the far north. The elation swells to see unexpected remnants from home without any buildup and anticipation, just pure spontaneity and surprise. We rejoice with more mushrooms.

Like Amber, Lyle has a real reason to be in Alaska. His family lives in Anchorage. After a few days of weed, wine, and festivals, he disappears from our company and heads to the big city to see his family.

Durgan has no plans. He's a cat, stealthy and smooth within the groove. He packed his guitar too. He joins Colin and me, and now we are three. We stick out our thumbs and head back to home base at Dragnet.

The summer is starting. The moon is jealous of the sun and the light will soon be replacing the reflection. When we first arrived a few weeks ago, this campground had about ten campers. It has quickly turned into a small city. Ten tents became twenty, then thirty, and then clusters of tents congeal like stardust to form our galaxy. Trails become trodden between the sites, factions begin to link to form a larger organism, breathing in synchronicity with the forest and the universe.

The purity of this playground spreads a benevolent energy, which acts as a contagion to its inhabitants. It must be something secreted directly from the trees. It is in the air. We are all in this together. You, me, Cole, our neighbors, we all arrive at the gates of the fish kingdom, but there are no fish here to meet us.

As the Earth swings around the sun to the month of June, I wonder if I should start hitchhiking over to Soldotna to look for Unko. I still have time if I leave now.

Durgan's guitar strings reverberate in the campfire glow, as we sit encircled on our logs, chatting and drinking. An older, salty man comes waltzing through our intimate environs. He walks briskly, head down only showing us the brim of his hat. He struts through the area like he lives here. He knows the trees, and he knows the paths. He walks up to our fire and stops. He turns his head slightly north to address those of us who have abruptly ended our conversations and now stare at him.

"Who wanna come work for me?" his croaky voice emanates from the other side of the crimson firelight, casting shadows upon his face. We all look around at each other, not sure how to read this situation. Naturally, Colin is the first to speak.

"Who are you and what do you do?"

"I got a boat and I'ma get some fish!" His condescending tone sends ripples through our blissful ignorance. "Come down to the dock and I'll show yas."

The thorny conversation dwindles and his voice fades into the background. We return to our own self-involved discussions. He startles our attention back to him when he announces his departure.

"I'ma gonna leave now, kay." He walks between us and the fire, turns back and says "Oh, I'm Jim."

Over the next several days, people from our forest go to his boat, but they all come back to the party instead, rejecting his offer of employment. No one seems interested. This is nonsense to me, why wouldn't they jump at this opportunity? I am excited to learn that no one has taken the job, it still sits like a bright shiny rock in the middle of a dune, waiting to be snatched. I must see for myself. I am going to visit Jim.

I hitch for half an hour and arrive at his pier. The walkway to his boat is rickety and wooden, riddled with splinters, stained dark from the tinge of salty sea water. The dock and the vessel match perfectly, like the boat and the plank were built around one another in a bygone era, in contrast to the neighboring Fiberglas and metal boats.

The short plank stretches out to his boat, hanging ten-feet above the low tide. A sensation tingles my spine that says I may never return to shore after I enter this surreal sea-craft. Jim pokes his head out of the cabin from his boat on the other side and grumbles in my direction.

"Hhhuhhhmm," Captain Jim says, his head hanging low, just like it was on that night around the fire.

Jim motions for me to cross the plank and follow him on board. He turns his back to me and disappears down a flight of stairs. I follow. There is a small puddle of water next to the wall that is starting to collect into a pool. Jim bends down to adjust a cloth he has twisted between the floorboards. "Don't worry about that, nothin." These are the first coherent words he has said to me today.

Jim is living in the past. His wooden boat creaks like an old shack. The newest part of his boat is a large wooden steering wheel, acting like the centerpiece at a dinner table. A three-meter spool holds a coiled net at the stern of the craft. If you've never mingled with pirates, stern is aft and aft is the back, why they make this so confusing I will never know. Wrapped up in the spool is the net, the lifeline, the sole purpose for this craft to be a fishing boat. It brings in the haul.

Against all better judgements, I take the job with Captain Jim as his deck hand. I don't know what a deckhand is or does. I don't know anything about boats, fish, or the water. As the salty dogs call it, I am green.

The interview process was just a visit to the campsite, asking if anyone wants to meet him at 6 am the next day. He's not particular. Three days later, it seems that I am the only one interested in the job.

It will be just him and me, so thankfully Jim stocks a lot of beer. We go out into the Cook Inlet for 24-hr stretches. We throw the net in the water, sit and wait for a few hours, drink beer, and try to understand each other while the fish run into the net. Dumb fish.

It's quite boring, until we start pulling in the net. Jim shows me how to jerk the net and break the gills, releasing the fish from his trap. We pluck the salmon onto the floor and thump them with a baseball bat. Jim shoots a few with his pistol, which might explain the hole in the floorboards I saw earlier. Once dead, we kick the fish down a hole.

After a few hundred of these, I learn the limits of my grip, and realize that I will need stronger gloves. Hell, I need stronger hands. My fists ache outward from their cores and now just dangle, limp and lifeless. They are useless and dead. I fear permanent damage. This job is not for me.

We float for six nights and seven days on drunken Captain Jim's holy wooden boat, navigating to the blotches we see on his fish finder. On the seventh day, I muster the courage.

"Jim, I suggest you look for another deck hand." He gives me a stern but steady gaze to see if I am sincere. He mumbles something under his breath. The only word I hear is *shore*. It appears he is unhappy to be going back to Kenai, but I miss my friends, my grip, and stable land.

I'm not sure about his plans, but I have some of my own and they no longer involve this shitty ship. After hours of uncomfortable silence, except for the roar of the engine, we dock at a seiner boat and unload our fish. After a few more hours helping Captain Jim mend his net, he climbs inside the boat's sleeping quarters while I head to the highway with my thumb out and return to my tent.

I've been gone for a week when I walk back into the Dragnet campsite. Things have changed over this short time, but at least my tent is in the same place I left it. I see Colin and we talk over beers and campfire light.

"Durgan went over to Seward two days ago." This comes as a shock to me, we never got to say goodbye, but things are like that when the wind blows heavy.

"Everyone's fishing on set-netters. I work there now too!" We discuss how I can get on his crew and then resign ourselves to dreams.

The drift-netting I did with Captain Jim was floating around, finding a spot, and throwing the net where we think the fish might be. We were drifting. Set-netting is close to shore, with dozens of fixed nets, anchored by buoys floating in the bay. Instead of hefty ships battling the sea, we now use speedy skiffs that skitter between the nets before we return to the dock. We go out at every low-tide when the water is less choppy, and the nets are high and stable. We work for six hours, wait another six hours for the tide to recede, and then work six more hours. Repeat. For weeks.

These are sleepless times; we are on the Alaskan summer schedule now. The tides don't coordinate with us either, it's usually low tide and time to work during the few hours of darkness we get at night, but we're learning how to take power naps between the tides.

After Jim's boat, my grip could barely hold a pencil. I can still feel the slow death of my ligaments, deep down inside my digits, but it is now only an echo of pain, rather than being in the forefront. The aches are now brandished to muscle memory. The net and I started out as bitter rivals a month ago, but after the many days of strain, my grip has come back as superhuman. I can now wring blood from stones if the need arises.

The skiff captains know two important things: firstly, the fish are only here to spawn for a short span, then they don't come back for a full year. Secondly, when the canneries open, we are all getting the hell off these boats and this crazy sleep routine. We are temporary and expendable. We need to get these fish caught, that is our purpose. We are slaves to our circumstance. Sorry fish, you must die. Thump.

The docks begin to overflow as the fish make their way to processing. Dragnet enforces their rule that if we camp here, we will work for them. We follow the same cycle as the fish, only we are led by different hooks.

On dry land, we try to stabilize, to sleep, and to revive our social lives. Our forest home has grown in numbers and in personality. When the summer started, we built our kitchens, the campfire pits, and the latrines. Our neighbors solidified into a tribe, and our commune melted into the forest.

The masses are here now. There are thirty new campsites in our forest, soaking up every available spot. We can no longer dance around and breathe the fresh air. Even our hacky-sack spot has a car parked in the way.

These people must have been waiting in the lower forty-eight for the signal. They missed all the fun leading up to this moment, but they are here now. They are considerate, but they haven't been living here for the last two months. We welcome these new faces and turn them into new friends while sharing our forest amenities.

The new forest people also come with cars, which permits the luxury of moving up and down the peninsula without using our thumbs. Ironically, our work schedules don't allow for the freedom of travel anymore.

With this many people in the vicinity, Colin and I don't interact much. Our tents are still neighboring, but that is where our courtesies and our boundaries split. He smokes pot all day and I drink vodka every night. We don't mix.

The beer cans that used to line our kitchen shelves have been replaced with bars of soap, dirty towels and rubber gloves. The party has moved to the right, while we buckle down and turn on the lights.

It's time for us to tuck our tails and assimilate, to get to work and make this place operate. It's last call and they're passing out the brooms.

The cannery life is not as glamorous as we were led to believe. Every morning we awake at 5:30 am, throw on stinky dirty clothes, sometimes wet with slime, and meet our crew at the chow hall for breakfast.

By 6 am we are all at our stations either cutting off heads or spooning out the fish guts. We don't rotate stations much, they want us to become supreme experts of these monotonous tasks. I became a tenth-level black belt fish scooper after six minutes on day one.

We charge ahead until dinner at 7 pm. They give us the option to work for three more hours, leaving at 10 pm. I tried that once, but I don't see the point of that suffering. I leave after dinner, usually a generous 14-hour shift. I want for endless days of mushroom festivals, hacky-sacks, and rusted roots, but those moments have faded away.

Months pass. The seiner boats bring smaller loads and the private fisherman disappear from the docks. The work days shorten in partnership with the diming sunshine and the darkening nights. As the fishing season ends, our friends all slowly disappear into the world.

We could go home too, but that doesn't sound like fun for any of us. We are too wild, and home is a destination that we've all seen before. We linger around our campsites, hoping to push the summer to its final breath. We desperately search for the vibe and the energy we had so many months ago, but the cannery sucked that life from us and from our environment. We are the last ones here and we have no plans, no homes, and nowhere to go.

Colin and I have come together after months of not speaking. We are making plans as a team again. Nine of us are left in the campground, with three cars that can take us wherever we may wish to go.

The foreman points us towards the next largest body of water, The Prince William Sound, to the city of Valdez. The fishing season there lasts into October, it doesn't die so rudely at the end of August like it just did in Kenai. Upon hearing this, we immediately begin packing.

We are moving the party at daybreak.

15

Fumbling in the Dark

2

T he Alaskan seasons ebb and flow like the tides we rode on the fishing skiffs at the beginning of the summer. The fish are nearly done spawning, and their migratory patterns are changing. We must also migrate. We are acutely aware, there's a pressure of despair, the winter is looming. We only wish to perpetuate the summer. We follow the salmon to new waters.

Camping life on the Kenai Peninsula is lush with freedom in wide open spaces, without concern, skipping through forest villages that stretch up and down the Cook Inlet. The long hitchhiking trips lead to vibrant festivals, free of constraints. Kenai is a permanent party in lasting lightness.

When the light fades with the summer sun, our forest friends decay into the woodwork, disappearing from our summer, reappearing in somewhere else's season. I am with Cole, my original travel partner. We've been together since the start, but we have grown to a group of nine and have nothing to do. We are on this ship together, and we sense the winter like a dark cloud on a turbulent sea. We have a mutual mission to find a way to get some cash and create some options once this summer ends.

The drive from Kenai to Valdez first goes north to Anchorage, Alaska's largest and most modern city. Then it turns east for four more hours until the mountains come into view. Then we go south another four more hours and begin our final leg into Valdez.

Outside the car, the view is engulfed by trees and glaciers. Inside the car, beers and smokes are engulfed by us. We binge drink until the final hour. It is September, the tail end of summer. The fires are fading, but the mountain peaks still loom, and the waterfalls and streams still flow with remnants of the summer. Driving through this beautiful state, we absorb every ray of sunshine even though the windows of daylight are closing.

We arrive in Valdez at 10 pm. It is already dark, signaling that the endless twilight-dawn and long summer nights are gone. The air is warm, and the night is calm. We are at the end of a long road, having driven through jagged mountains and icy glaciers, and now arriving at a city perched alone on a bedrock by the sea.

The activity in Valdez is concentrated at the small boat harbor. The road to the canneries is along a spit of land, a tiny peninsula jutting into the bay. This horse-shoe shaped road separates the harbor from the waves that follow the big tankers. The spit serves as a barrier island dedicated to the harvest of fish. This is cannery row, there's no mystery where we need to go.

Halfway around the bend in the road, between the fish processing plants and the town, sits Hippy Hill. Like a lighthouse, it is a viewpoint across the water, while the other side of the hill overlooks the small boat harbor. The Hill is also the only place to camp that is near the canneries.

From the moment we kill our engines on top of The Hill, it becomes frantic. The calm and camaraderie of the road is replaced by a frantic need to find a home. This is not the forest, this is a rocky field of gravel a mere hundred feet across. Spaces are limited.

Twenty or thirty concrete slabs are spaced around the hilltop, indicating the dedicated camp spots for whomever may choose the plot. About half of the slabs are empty, while the other half are occupied by tents but without tenants. We are alone. Everyone must be working the final throngs of the salmon run.

We scramble, competing to find the best real-estate with views over the bay. My slab is in the corner, by the small patch of trees at the end. I look across the gravel and see Colin unpacking. We wave like it's the suburbs. My tent is only a five-foot square, but it is home. I throw my pack inside of my newly erect tent, zip my door, and enter my universe.

Four weeks pass, ample time to grow to appreciate this small, isolated town. Many of the workers dissipate as the stockpile of fish on the dock dwindles. My primary residence on this meager concrete slab on Hippy Hill quickly serves its purpose. It is time to upgrade. The air is getting chilly. With the out-flux of people, we can now move into the cannery housing.

The canneries provide rooms, but they are typically reserved for the captains and the supervisors. The rooms are part of trailers that will be hauled out of Valdez after the fishing season, to be reused at construction sites or pipeline spills. Each trailer has six rooms smaller than jail cells, with two beds and a narrow aisle between them. The rooms are shared, but the luxury of an actual bed, no matter how disgraced the state, is a blissful reprieve from and concrete and forest floors.

We've been working eighty hours a week for two months. The fish have started talking to me. My psychopathic tendencies towards Sally Salmon and all her sisters slowly returns. "I am back to avenge my mother!" I do, and five seconds later Colin hands me another fish.

These delusions help to pass the days, while the insanity of monotony oddly keeps us grounded. We value our free time but not so much our psyches.

After five more weeks of work and delirium, we all have enough dollars to do what we need, although I'm still uncertain what exactly that is. Everyone is in a hurry to get back south. Just as the Kenai folk had been, they are replete with urgency. I don't understand this drive, I'm complacent. I'm in no hurry.

19

I don't want to go home, and I can't go back to Spokane. I haven't thought much beyond Valdez, but the canneries are closing for the season. The chill in the wind signals that winter is on the horizon, and I haven't yet mapped my future.

We have experienced so much together, yet we always knew the summer would be temporary. Our clan of nine becomes seven, then four, and then dwindles to just me and my old buddy Cole.

A crossroads is upon us and we are taking different forks. Colin wants to return to the known universe to share his winter with those we left back in the triangle of Seattle, Spokane, and Walla Walla. That trap does not interest me anymore. It has only proven to lead to my destruction. I will buckle down in Valdez in what will be just another form of escape.

My roots tremble when Colin leaves. It fills me with the same dread I felt on the highway with Amber. He is my original travel partner and the last of the masses from the summer, except for me, I am still here. Nine becomes one - but will again become many. I look forward to creating a new past with a new crew. Colin is gone.

The Sugarloaf Bar and Restaurant is familiar. It has been our sanctuary away from the cannery for the last six weeks, a place to mingle and integrate. It absorbed any free time we had between the fish guts and the camp life. It was a natural transition for me to get a job washing dishes here after everyone else left for the lower states.

They offer a room and board deal, they'll put me up and feed me. The hotel is just across the parking lot from the bar, and the rooms are devoid of tourists this late in the season. I can wash dishes for the winter, I've done it before. I know this path, it is laid clearly at my feet, I know what I must do.

The Sugarloaf smells of sawdust, sweat, and mildew, tinged with a hint of raw fish and beer. The paint and wood are peeling from rough winters, but that same winter chill has also preserved the colors to retain their barn-red hues and white handrails.

There are two sets of stairs: the left one goes to the restaurant and the right one goes to the bar. I always go right. Past the bar and the tables, another set of stairs descends to a small stage and a handful of pool tables under two mounted moose heads. A spacious balcony overlooks the main road coming into town, beckoning fisherman and travelers to stand on its terrace and look out at the mountains, while enjoying nachos and alcohol.

My life has become benign since the dissolution of the nine. The excitement has drained. Washing dishes is only slightly more glamorous than slagging fish, but it will do for now. It gives me a place to sleep and a meal to eat.

My new brethren are avid thrill seekers – they jump off cliffs, climb frozen waterfalls with ice axes, and jump their snowmobiles over the highway before heading back to town for a casual cup of cocoa.

They are transplanted, but they are local. They know why they are here. Maybe they'll sway me, I'm not sure how I ended up her. I dance upon the last remnants of summer energies and share vibrant stories with my new friends. We watch the days get shorter with each sunset.

If someone had told me that the Alaskan winters are not only cold, but extremely dark and depressing, I might have followed Colin out of this hole. My only relief is my proximity to the bar and its artificial light in these nighttime hours that extend into dark days. The earth is flipping and leaving us out in the cold.

Winter Warnings | *December*

Reba is Crow Indian, but her pale skin and curly brown hair conceal her heritage. Her folksy songs sing to the working man, solidifying her position and her role within this microcosm of the Sugarloaf Bar. Reba has connections. When cabin fever starts to boil and the rats come out of the floorboards, she is there to squash them with her dulcimer.

I go to the bar every night to hear her sing, as I have done for the last two months. Her angelic voice melts the frost from my brittle mind. We become close. Tonight, after the crowd thins, the bar closes, and the dim lights brighten, we become even closer. Reba and I are not content to go to our homes. Our energies are entwined, and all is right.

"I don't see why the night should end," I say to Reba. "I live just on the other side of this parking lot." We giggle at the proximity.

"Let me finish this and pack my guitar." She slams her glass of merlot and hastily rummages through her gear. We quickly disappear, down the stairs and across the lot to my waiting hotel room.

At 7 am, there is a knock at the door that jolts us both awake. I tell Reba, "I'm not expecting company, but this could be anyone."

"Don't answer it! Remember, I'm married." I now remember this tidbit that was thrown in amongst the moans last night, but during that inopportune time, I chose to ignore it. I never anticipated him knocking on the door this early in the morning. How did he find us?

Another series of knocks ensues. "Come to the door!" It's a grumbly woman's voice that I recognize from my job interview. It's not Reba's husband, it's the owner of the restaurant and bar.

The owner holds all the power, she employees me and all my friends, including Reba. The owner is also the hand that feeds and provides me with a free hotel room. She comes into the restaurant for wine sometimes, she seems fine, but she also has a reputation for being ruthless and mildly psycho.

"D-do you-do wh-what do you last n-night?"

"What?" It's too early, I can't think straight. I didn't know she stammered and can't form sentences when she's anxious. I am asleep in my room, it's 6am! Why is she knocking on my door?

"S-sleeping, ups-upstairs," she stutters.

"No, I'm sleeping here," I clarify, anxious to return to that precise activity at this ungodly hour.

"No-nn-no, *I'm* Sle-sleeping," she says, pointing at the ceiling, her hand now shaking.

"Ok, so why are you not sleeping now? What do you want?" Through her grumbly, shaky replies, I discern that she lives in the room directly above mine and that we made too much noise and kept her awake all night.

"J-just g-go! OUT! Two hours!" She turns and walks away, leaving me to wonder if she's serious.

Reba was listening, and she understands the owner's malady. They have known each other for years. Reba translates. Apparently, the owner frequently fires people as a show of power, and her decision is always unshakable.

I have two hours to exit the premises. It's cold outside. This is worrisome. The Alaskan winters are not known to be kind to the homeless. I have until nightfall to figure out where I am sleeping tonight, or I will default to an icy meadow where I may never awaken from certain hypothermia.

The Alaskan summertime teaches and preaches controlled homelessness. This is built into the Kenai plan. Last year, Ed and Jaybird were sent by the universe to make sure I could live to tell my tale. This summer, Colin and I embarked on a path with no clear residence, but home always felt near and there was never fear. Now it all leads me here.

I have been without a home or a plan a few times previously, history is repeating, and I am not adapting. When I left the Marines as a shell of a soul, I found my psyche shattered. Gateways led down slippery slopes until there were none left to explore. I'm grateful Gavin showed me that I was standing at the wrong door, and that Ethan showed me a new one.

This time, though, the thrill turns to fright. I can't just sleep outside if it comes to that. The cosmic ribbon always provides, but you must also feed the beast or the demons will rise.

Reba and her husband are very newly separated. She evicted herself from her own home just last night, in fact. For the first time in her life, Reba doesn't have anywhere to sleep either. We are homeless together.

We are now freed from these constrictions. We can focus purely on ourselves, but we are also free of the finer things like shelter, warmth, and security.

During the winter months, most of the locals head to Colorado or Hawaii. Their houses are left to brave the weather alone. The cold freezes the pipes and kills the dogs, while the snow collapses the rooftops.

It is equally imperative for them to have someone tend their homes as it is for us to have a home. It is a natural synergy, allowing Reba and I to couch surf for any of the potential hosts that allow us to stay. We bounce through other people's houses for two months as the snow buries the buildings and the darkness envelops the valley.

Our window of daylight is collapsing like the curtain closing the show. It's time to go home to sleep, to weep, to reconcile the skeletons and look deep inside the soul.

The First Immersion

3

Halfway through my first desolate winter, long after the tourists and hip fishies have left, the winds come subtly to rest. All that remains in this once vibrant village of Valdez are the alcoholics, the Christians and the hardcore mountain men, which arguably could fall into either of the two previous categories.

Most everyone has the insight to work their day at the pipeline and promptly return home, lock the doors, and spend time with their families. My kin and I seek additional stimuli outside of core business hours.

The sun makes quick daily peeks over the mountain tops for a few hours, but otherwise the gloom of darkness obscures us from the world. Valdez only has about two hours of twilight, regardless of the season. The summers have a quick dusk near midnight that breaks seamlessly into dawn and long days. The winters are reversed. The noon sunrise quickly melts into the dark night before we've even finished our lunches. During these cold winter months, we are forced to wait twenty hours until the sun makes another encore appearance across the mountain tops.

The landscape of this forested village is now transformed into the opposite of her former summer glory. The Chugach Mountains land-lock us towards the bay, trapping all precipitation overhead, which spills over like a bowl when the clouds burst. In the summer, these clouds sprinkle the trees with misty rain that is romanticized in all the man-tames-wild novels. When the mercury drops in the winter, the overhead precip freezes and buries the town in snow.

It's November and the snow is late to the show, but like pent up frustration, the sky expulses its contents all at once. Within seven days, an eleven-foot accumulation of snow buries houses up to their rooftops.

The local transportation changes from pickup trucks to snowmobiles. Snow plows attack the only road into town, but all distinguishable landmarks are buried. Thankfully, the town is small, and the traffic is thin.

I failed to pack my portable snowmobile in my backpack last spring when I first left for the Alaskan wilderness, not realizing I would still be here for the winter and not realizing what kind of a winter it would be. I will need to find a hobby.

It has been a month since I worked at the Sugarloaf, or anywhere. I need a solution. I am not worried, not yet, despite not having a job, money or any real prospects. After five weeks of house-sitting, I land a stable job that comes with a room deal again. These are increasingly convenient while I am battling homelessness.

I now cook breakfast and lunch at the Glacier Restaurant and Hotel, about a ten-minute walk from The Sugarloaf. Like all establishments in this town, business at the Glacier is slow during these winter months. I might cook half a dozen eggs on a busy morning, and my lunch specials are mostly wasteful.

Just as I find a home, Reba also finds a place on her own too. When we first met, we spontaneously became homeless together, and now we both end that cycle with suspiciously eerie timing. The town is small, we won't drift very far from one another, but for now, the intimacy of joint-homelessness fades.

It doesn't take long to learn to cook the menu at The Glacier. All the meals are the same essential items in different orders. Any homeless vagabond can apply heat and turn them into edibles. Beef, chicken or fish – with either potatoes, noodles, or rice. I got this.

I've made a connection with one customer who always comes in on his way to the pipeline. He's young like me, but we are very different. He has taken a different road to this restaurant where we now sit and discuss our deepest perspectives about life, love, happiness, and the ways of the heavens.

Beau is my liaison to the spiritual world. As his name implies, he is a handsome man who is halfway through his twenties. Not one of his short dark hairs is out of place. If he were an actor, he would be in one of those shampoo commercials where they whip their heads in slow motion, exposing their shimmering follicles that always fall back in line.

Beau tucks his T-shirt into his jeans, giving him an air of class that the rest of us lack. He is sobriety and purity personified. He is slender and well kept, but not well versed in the ways of the world. Beau was born and raised in Valdez, a true small-town staple. He hasn't explored much outside of this small town, but he doesn't need to. His mind lives within his Bible, which is never far from his reach.

After closing the Glacier, I invite Beau to partake in the after-shift custom. "Let's go get a beer!" I say to Beau. It was at this point I realize Beau is special, unique in the land of perpetual night, a resistance fighter to anything adverse.

"No, let's go to church." Beau is a proud member of the Robe Lake Apostolic Pentecostals. They're a devout sect of Christianity that should want me nowhere near its doors. I fit a different mold.

In dynamic opposition to Beau – is Bud. He is my liaison to the after-hours, the underworld, the heathens that shake in the night. Bud drinks beer, Bud smokes bud, but he knows nothing of Beau's Bible.

Bud is cheery and always smiling, but at nearly fifty, his hair is gray and thinning. He has passed his prime, while I am still looking for mine.

His Santa-style beer belly stretches his T-shirt taught, while tucked into his jeans just like Beau. But unlike Beau, Bud's gut obstructs any efforts at adding class to his appearance. It doesn't detract, everyone is naturally drawn to his cheery face anyway.

Bud is also an ex-convict who was nabbed fifteen years' prior for stealing a car. His outward appearance is well kept, but his interior needs some housekeeping. I often think that he got caught on purpose since he is also gay. Three squares, a bed, and living with a hundred manly men? He may have found pleasant ways to spend his time. Now he is back in the real-world bartending where I cook breakfast.

One night, just as the bar was closing and we were voicing our misery of perpetually dark days, he looks at me convincingly and says something so modest yet profound, it changes the course of my life.

Despite his flaws, Bud will be my catalyst, my slingshot that will utter a few simple words, sending me into orbit around the planet. His words are wise, infinitely profound and motivating, yet reveal the simplest truth.

Bud is a rooted transient who got stuck for the winter just like me. In this touristy town, it is important to acknowledge the ebb and the flow of the population and census with the seasons. The summer brings the energy, while the winter brings introspection.

Bud is the horned devil on my left shoulder, while Beau has the halo on my right. These two influences work in concert together, complementary and complete. They work through me without needing to be acquainted with each other.

There are two things to do in Valdez during the winter: drink beer and go to church, but I learned that it is frowned upon to do both on the same night. This ping-pong battle between opposing venues lasts for a few weeks until I realize I am spending more time with Beau at church than with Bud at the bar. Valdez is a place where competing worlds unite, but I will also soon learn that the same applies to all of Earth and her humanity.

The sermons are in the pastor's house, upon which he erected a monstrous white cross at the apex of his roof, seeming to call all towards its message. I wonder what it would look like with that cross ablaze, atop his house. It would create an entirely different vibe.

There's an external entrance to the basement, where he has his pews lined up. It is well lit from within, throwing light out of the windows onto the banks of snow. Like a flashlight shining in the corners of our closets, our evils are illuminated.

I am always uncomfortable entering the belly of this beast. Each time, I attempt to enter unannounced and sit quietly in the back pew just to observe. This has always proven impossible since the Pentecostal sessions are highly interactive.

About twenty boys sit on one side of the aisle and about ten girls sit on the other side, their hands in their laps, prim and proper. The pastor paces through this gender divide, preaching his message of babble-on.

Their church is ordinary enough, but their beliefs confound me. The females can't cut their hair and they are forbidden to adorn themselves with Jewelry or makeup. They must always wear dresses. The men are also held to high standards, but it is much easier for them to forego the jewelry, the makeup and the dresses. They must keep their hair trim and respectable, while not adorning crosses or false idolatry.

It is forbidden to watch television, since technology is the spawn of Satan, spouting nonsense to tempt God's children into lustful temptations. They also think the earth is only six thousand years old and don't believe in science.

They study the Bible quite literally with no room for interpretation. Disobeying the written word is a sin, or at least a religious misdemeanor. I am a smoker and that is a desecration of my temple, an apparent felony for my soul. They know nothing of my sordid past, but even my haggard self is eligible for redemption.

On the road to heaven, there is no gray area, no ambiguity, and no mercy. The show is sold-out, and The Holy Ghost is only admitting those with VIP backstage passes. Their sermons remind me of something I saw in the backwoods bayou in Louisiana back in the Corps.

"Jesus lordy amen hallelujah, come on now!" Clapping, chanting, dancing and speaking in tongues are requisite at these thrice weekly gatherings. I've never heard someone speak in tongues before, not up close. It seems silly, like they've all learned the same language, but they don't care that everyone's words don't match.

"Who amongst us has never been saved, oh my! Go ahead and raise your hands up there, fresh faces!" I am not fond of audience participation, but he is standing five feet away and looking directly down at me.

"What do you want out of this life, young man?"

"Same as you, I presume." He starts pacing again.

"You gotta want it, yessir. Reach out and take it. So I ask again, who amongst us want to be *saved*?"

Timidly and slowly, I raise my hand. He puts his hand on my forehead and commands me to speak in tongues. I give it my best attempt, but it is like being hypnotized at the county fair, when I was swiftly escorted off stage for not falling under the hypnotist's spell.

Every time I open my mouth to let ancient Aramaic roll from my tongue, it just sounds like "looma looma bumpa bumpa." Jesus just doesn't want to speak through my jabbering tongue, while others make it seem effortless to abandon control. I am aware of each syllable and can faithfully make my mouth say whatever I wish. This restraint would have been useful during earlier phases of my life.

The pastor isn't nearly as dismissive or forgiving as the hypnotist, although I suppose their professions do share cultist similarities. The preacher proclaims that all I need is a good cleansing. The devil has my tongue and its filth needs to be washed away.

"Let's take you to the lake to be washed anew, reborn and ready to start again! Let's get you baptized in the name of the Holy Ghost." I am told this will grant me a do-over at life.

The pastor startles me by putting his hand on my shoulder. "Oh! We're go... we're going *now*?" I stutter like the Sugarloaf owner. A mild debate ensues as I am ushered to my feet. I make excuses about the chilly winter water, my lack of proper clothing, all the while just wanting to tell him "NO! I DO NOT WANT TO GO!"

He insists there is no reason to wait and appeals to my sense of spontaneity. I agree, I'm not doing anything tonight and he's driving. The entire congregation is in fervent support of my baptism. We pack into four cars and drive a mile down the street to Robe Lake.

I'm only twenty-three years old, but I have accumulated a closet-full of sins in search of instant gratification. The impulses sustain me. I hope that in this situation, here and now with this priest, a brighter light will spark than those I've before had to extinguish.

The dark Alaskan night shrouds everything within earshot. Echoes bounce off the still blackness. The lake is dark, a few glimmering lights from neighboring houses remind us that though isolated, we are not wholly alone.

We are below a lonely and crooked street light, standing on a gravel bank at the edge of the water, next to a small waterlogged dock that is slowly slipping towards the bottom of the lake. The congregation is in a half-moon on the shore like the crescent in the sky. I stand with them, still in denial that this gathering is for my benefit and for my rebirth.

The pastor grabs my hand again, and we walk towards the water so that he may perform his miracle. With his other hand flat on my back, we turn away from the congregation, all whom stand motionless, eyes fixated in witness.

I traipse clumsily, careful to not become ensnared by reeds and weeds. It all happens so fast. The air is crisp and quiet. The cold water penetrates my jeans and I instantly want this experience to end. We walk further out until the cold water rises past our waists. It's fucking cold! ...*if I may now speak in tongues.*

"Are you ready?" I look at him curiously. He was not this accommodating when he rushed me out of the church. Is this my last chance to say no?

Sandwiching my torso between his hands, he utters some last words about The Father, The Son, and The Holy Ghost. I plug my nose and back my weight upon his hand so that he may dunk me into the frigid water.

In my youth, I was told
That the world itself would unfold,
Into the laps of yours and mine,
For the whole of human kind.

But with the years, and all our tears,
What was left behind-
Was the soul, the spirit,
and the great divine.

I submerge to find mine.

Gateways

4

I believed it all.

When I was young, I believed in god, guns and bubble gum. I believed in America and talking mice, in Santa Claus and Jesus Christ. I believed in everything I was told, in society and being bold. With faith in my congregation, I rejoiced in god, race, and nation. Policemen were my friends, so I was taught, and there were no politicians that could be bought. I knew Santa Claus was just a little game, but we couldn't just praise it all in the good lord's name.

That little boy is dead. He doesn't believe that anymore. He followed his choices down dark tunnels, searching for the most basic, instinctual, and primal drives. The quest for experience cut a path through life and innocence, defining the phases, dealing that little boy a death blow.

I've been out of high-school for a year now, I'm on my own. I can't turn back. I've already signed the papers, passed the tests, said my goodbyes and boarded the plane. It's time to see who I am.

When I land at the airport, they put me in a bus with blackened windows and fifteen other people I've never seen before in my life. The uniformed men yell at us, "Put your heads in your laps! No looking out the windows!"

It's impossible to see through black windows anyway. I sit motionless and petrified. My head is in my lap just as the angry man instructs.

The bus pulls out of the parking lot and we drive for a mere fifteen minutes. The depot is close to the airport, there is no time to adjust. We arrive.

"Get out! Get out NOW! Feet on the footprints! GET OUT!" With my head tucked low, I am shepherded out of the bus with the other throngs of confused youths. I plant my feet into the outlines of footprints painted yellow on the pavement. "Roll Call!"

We are rushed into the receiving area as other buses arrive. "STRIP! Strip down to your skivvies!"

"What are skivvies?"

One by one, we are invasively deloused with white powder and handed our new clothes and transition to the next line to get our heads shaved. I already shaved my head at home last week, except for a little Hari Krishna pony tail emanating from the middle of my head. They can take that if they must.

The next three days and three nights pass by in a whirlwind devoid of custom, as we prepare for our new normality. The days are filled with examinations, immunizations, orientations, and indoctrinations. During the endless hours in between, we sit crisscross-applesauce on the pavement, avoid eye contact, and await our next instructions.

For the next sixteen weeks, we are part of a social experiment without a control group. We are introduced to structure, cohesion and routine. I don't like this. I want to be skating my barn ramp. I can't run down to the corner store and buy some smokes, I can't order a pizza or party with my friends. Clearly, I can't have the company of women, a joy that I only discovered earlier this year.

This is the US Marine Corps Basic and Combat Training, also called Boot Camp. I'm here to be broken down and rebuilt in your image. Military training breaks even the biggest of men, so it is fortunate that I am average. Recruits come in all shapes and sizes, cultures, nationalities and backgrounds. We are thrown into a cultural caldron and stirred with the seasonings of structure and strangeness.

I've joined the biggest gang in the world and have a hundred and twenty new brothers in arms. Our gang includes cowboys from Texas, jocks that I typically avoid, and real gangsters from Los Angeles who were court sanctioned to enlist. We look for common ground to unite us in this battle to survive.

They teach me how to kill. I certify as rifle expert and master close combat with knives and other deadly tools. The academics are unchallenging. We learn the history of the Corps and which carrots on a stick we should follow.

From my toes to my face and down through my core, I am being transformed. Respect, Honor, dignity – these are my new favorite things, my creed. The drill instructors tell me this frequently, thus it must be true.

It is an unfortunate fact that only half of us will graduate and claim the title of United States Marine. We've lost half the people we started with, but I am one of the few, the proud. We sing this in cadence at graduation just prior to being shipped around the country to our different primary schools.

Some of my brothers stay here at Camp Pendleton to endure what is essentially an eternal boot camp, the Marine Corps Forced Recon, one of the world's elite fighting forces. I say goodbye to my grunt buddies. My orders are to fix radios in Memphis, Tennessee.

The months toil into years, as I perform my duties sweating in the deep south. I do this for my country, bound by contract and by oath. In return, I get food, a bed, and a paycheck. I am a good Marine, but a bad civilian. They shouldn't let me out of my cage.

Within the walls of this military base, I am a spit-shined and proper soldier, at attention and saluting. When I don't have guard duty, I go out with four other guys: two skinheads from Georgia, the son of a grand wizard in the Tennessee Ku Klux Klan, and a guy from Jersey. The Marine corps doesn't see skin color, they see people as either dark green and light green. My friends have all mostly reformed, although the skinhead is always angry at everyone.

I'm not sure where I fit in. I'm skate punk with a penchant for finding the path less trodden, and that path has led me here. Life has judged me guilty by association, but the associations are what breathes me life. I've made some friends, but I've also made some enemies.

This is Memphis, this is Beale Street and Sun Records. This is blues and the home of the kings, Elvis, BB and Dr. Martin Luther. We only come down to Beale if there's nothing else to do.

Our preferences are more nefarious. Memphis has thriving underground punk scene. This is our thing, far away from the masses. All the meanest shows are at the Antenna Club, it's a good place to evaporate angst. The Antenna also has the most lenient drinking policy. I'm only nineteen, but they let me use my friend's driver's license to buy beer. We're both bald, close enough. We are young marines, getting rowdy and going to mosh pits. We all cope however we can.

When we don't want to drive thirty minutes into Memphis, we just go to the shitty little strip club a few miles from base. We've gotten to know the girls well, they like the Marines more than the Navy boys. I'm usually the last one out of the bar and I don't have a car, so I always stumble back to base alone on foot.

There's a quaint residential area that I pass on these midnight strolls back to base. I like to hobble through here and set off the car alarms. These people shouldn't have normal lives while we are bound by codes.

I'm also a vandal and a thief. I kick over fences and rummage through cars. I steal toolboxes and spray paint doors in the night. This life outside of the concertina wire and armed guards is just make-believe. None of this is real, it doesn't matter if I break things. The military will protect me if I can get back inside our walls. Like a kid's game of tag, behind the base I am safe.

It doesn't take long for the police to catch on, or for me to walk into their trap. They know exactly what I am doing. I can't hide in the shadows or the bushes. I am getting drunk, going to the strip club, and fucking shit up on the way home. They get the reports.

There's one cop that always comes into the club and checks our identification just to harass us. He knows I'm too young to drink, and he also knows my route home. Last night he was waiting for me on the edge of my stomping grounds. Parked on the curb, he flashes his lights and waves me over. I think about running, then tripping over a plant, my face hitting the dirt, and waking up with him standing over me. I choose not to do that.

Instead, I wobble across the street to see what he wants. He can't prove I'm a vandal, but he gives me a ticket for drinking under the legal drinking age and puts me in a cell for the night.

This morning I was called in to see the judge, which may or may not have worked in my favor. The judge threw the case out of court, under the condition that the issue is transferred to my Commanding Officer.

My C.O. is not amused and puts me in the brig for two weeks. I am devoid of privileges in a military jail, cohabitating with a handful of other petty offenders. We do little more than stare at each and clean things to pass the time. I seem to have the longest sentence, though. A few other marines come and go for various offenses, but they are all fresh faces when I leave.

Serving two weeks of soft-time feels like being grounded, but there are additional requirements. My C.O. is making me attend weekly Alcoholics Anonymous meetings. He also assigns me to go to inpatient rehabilitation to cleanse me of my alcoholism. Nah, I'm not ready for that, that's too much. I request another audience with my Commanding Officer, and with the Marine Corps legal departments.

"Sir, what happens if I choose not to go to treatment?" I ask at firm attention, chin up, chest out, shoulders back, stomach in, feet at forty-five degrees, and thumbs along my seams. My eyes are staring directly through my commanding officer. My voice is sincere, we are here because I requested this session. I seek information, but I must show proper protocol if I am to be taken seriously. This is a risk, he could put me back in the brig. I am certain that he already hates me.

"At ease, soldier," booms the colonel's voice. He sits down and smirks up at me.

This meeting is much more relaxed than the last time when he grounded me. Colonels have more important things to do than coddle a lowly enlisted soldier, but still, he gives me respect and makes me feel comfortable. This is refreshing; I didn't realize he was human.

"Look son, you got six months left, right?"

"Yes Sir."

"Then you got a choice to make." He pauses. I wonder if this is where I'm supposed to say something.

"You've been ordered to get in-patient treatment and attend AA meetings. As a Marine, I expect you to follow these orders."

"Yes sir."

"But here's the choice. The brass have been making cutbacks and giving early discharges. Most of my marines want to stay with the bond of the corps, but I don't need any men here that don't want to be here." That's me! He's talking about me!

"If you want to quit early, I have no reason to stop you. You'll still get an honorable discharge, but you can't reenlist." He looks at his legal team. "Is that right?"

"Sir, you are correct, sir." The two butter-bar lieutenants from the Navy JAG legal team say in unison.

"Sirs, what repercussions can I expect from this, what happens in the civilian world?" I'm looking at the lawyers, but the colonel doesn't let them respond.

"Son, we can't promise you anything out there. That's you against the jungle, without your brothers by your side. but you do what you have to."

"I have other brothers," I wanted to say, but lacked the courage. I tuck my chin and straighten my posture.

The colonel makes a few soft-handed jabs at my masculinity but I ignore them. I'm focusing on what I must be missing, but I am missing nothing. I'm not interested in reenlisting, that would defeat the point. This deal is indeed what I need.

I smile wide but keep my composure. I look at the JAG sirs and back at the Colonel. My Commanding Officer says sternly, "Will that be all, soldier?"

"Yes sir. Thank you, sir!" I return to attention, execute a salute crisp enough to chop wood, do an about-face and march out the door.

I am Marine corpse, a limp soul on a lifeless path. My time inside leaves me bemused and confused. It will take years to snap out of the wash and reconstruct my own beliefs atop of those that have just left me in a haze.

I hope I will never go to foreign lands and kill people, that shouldn't be anyone's path. I am just here to learn and see. I have done something that none of my friends have done and I feel special. Ooh Rah.

I must decide. One door takes me to rehab for alcoholism. It would allow me to see this path to its rightful end and not close any doors to my future. A second door takes me home to be with my friends, skate my ramp, see shows and have a party. That's a better idea, I'll do that. I sign my discharge papers, make my escape, and I am home for Christmas.

This Integration

5

My Marine Corps career ends in a joyous fizzle, but part of me will always be left behind. Once a marine, always. I've given a lot of myself away since I joined, sweating alongside my brothers in arms, but I have bigger plans.

The bus pulls up to Memphis station. I throw my rucksack in the bottom and climb up next to a window. It takes three-days to get home to Walla Walla, Washington, the land so nice they named it twice, the land of my birth.

When I return, I quickly realize that I am not the only one who has changed. In my years before the corps, before crossing the threshold into adulthood, I reveled in simplicity and alcohol. We all did.

Our core crew was a solid dozen, with some new faces that pop in and out like quarks, appearing ever so briefly and then disappearing again. Instead, the core crew has been whittled down to a few of my favorite people, plus a select few of the quarks that have now become constants.

I am a recently liberated US Marine, finally released from the thumb of Uncle Sam. I have no direction or clear path ahead. I've taken some demons with me, but I've found my celebration. I've returned from my service, still a young man, in my hometown again. I am gleeful to be a civilian.

I see some of my old friends and try to integrate back into my old life, but the party has moved, and my friends have scattered. After just a week visiting my parents, I decide to follow in the footsteps of my friends. I stuff all my possessions into my white Volkswagen Rabbit and move away. Again.

I need to see Gavin in Spokane. I need to make a connection that has been severed. I need to find my ground. He is a true constant. Gavin is the unassuming guy who everyone likes and invites into their home. He knows all the cool people and always goes to the best shows. He does the magic tricks at the parties and tells the knock-knock jokes. Gavin is a rock, a constant that the water flows around.

It's been eight years since we first met in the skate punk phase during high school. This was even before the Corpse. That is a third of a lifetime ago.

Gavin is a few inches taller and a year older, although infinitely wiser than me. His disproportionately large nose matches his big ears, but he's cool with that. His long blonde hair frames his kind eyes. He's physically strong too, with a steadfast loyalty. We follow the same trend lines; our paths are linked. It has just always been this way.

Gavin and I are now roommates. It starts with just us, but over the next six-months, we grow to a crew of eight people. Not all our new friends are on our apartment lease, but most of them have moved in anyway. We never really say "no" to anything. It's only a two-bedroom dump, but people sleep wherever they can.

While some of us get into chemicals to escape, Gavin's choice has always been strictly liquid, liquor, liqueur. The nectar of whiskey and cheap beer keeps his spirit vibrant, while the chemicals and needles solidify our hearts into crystal.

We don't mind the cockroaches so much or even the tight living constraints. We never sleep anyways and there is always someone around to talk to. I do, however, find it odd that even those on the lease can't pay for the lights yet there always seems to be funds for our illicit habits. That works too, though.

I don't want to work, but I must support my habits. The local steel foundry hires me to make metal molds of pliers, by rotating heavy casts in the fires of an enormous furnace.

It's hard, hot work, but it satiates my thirst. I'm on the graveyard shift with one other guy. Most nights, I'm the most productive employee in the company. But when I'm sober, I usually just sit huddled in the dark, holding my knees, rocking back and forth.

Spokane is my devil's playground. We party for endless nights that blend into days and then into more nights. My quest is nonstop, except for Wednesdays, of course. I search for that shiny thing on the trail, the one that lures me over the edge, into the mouth of the monster that I am addicted to.

The curiosity consumes me, the insight elevates me, the highs redeem me from my last world in the military. I have found a new demon to battle my old ones. Demons aren't monsters, or people, or weird beasts. They are the things that make us feel good, but we know are bad for us. They are the temptations that drag us down and try to change us, diverting us from the proper paths.

I feed my demons well. They fight the battles, making the choices between feeling good now - or feeling good later. These are dark days and high nights. The residual sentiments from the Marine Corps run deep, but the addiction runs even deeper. It is entangled with my being. It always wins.

If I fail to feed the hunger, the starvation is all-consuming. The hunger will always find food if I starve it long enough, even if it gorges upon the elements that construct me: my spirit, my person, my moods, my soul.

Week after week and month after month, I create a chemical imbalance to perpetuate a delusion of prosperity, but instead it is my own sanity that lacks substance. Through these deluded filters, the city is afire.

My weekends start on Thursday night and end on Tuesday, typically lasting five or six sleepless cycles. I sleep on Wednesdays. I am nearing the end of a downward spiral. I have slipped on the slope, through the gateways and into other gateways, and have become my own voodoo doll on pins and needles, spoons, herbs, and powders. There's good news though – I am immortal.

My finely sculpted Marine Corps body has withered away. My chiseled muscles have turned into a skeleton. I now fit the junkie mold. The day's only purpose is to feed the night, and life's only purpose is to not die.

Year One | Spring

Ethan and Amber have the same habits and routines as me. We are kindred minds. They are a sweet couple, bound like neurons firing all at once. They both fashion themselves with long brown hair, although Ethan's is much greasier. Amber is a goddess who doesn't fit this lifestyle. She is smart, sweet, beautiful, and stop that, she is Ethan's girl.

They know all the musicians in town and lurk in the shadows of the city's underbelly. Ethan is one of our unleased roommates. He lives with Gavin and me at the ironically named Casa del Sol Apartments. It is not the house of the sun.

Ethan contributes to rent, but not as a legal tinder and his payment is usually not in cash. He likes to play music, but he isn't very good. He likes to read, but only as a last option, and usually out loud. Much like Gavin, he entertains us constantly. He is smaller and shorter than I am, so that gives me power and comfort.

Ethan is one of my favorite lost souls. He plants an idea in my frizzled brain that a summer in Alaska is exactly the escape we need to clear these cobwebs. We may even come back as real people, free from our current compulsions, no longer outrunning storm clouds.

Things are going nowhere fast in this land of cockroaches and hot, hard work. Alaska is where the gods are, but even failing all spiritual revivals, we will at least come home with a pocket full of cash from fishing.

Amber was born in Alaska, she will be our safety net. She's staying with her family in Anchorage for the summer, but Ethan and I will go south and work in the salmon fisheries. We won't linger in the big city.

The three of us establish our timelines and coordinate our flight plans, but instead we book three different flights that are days apart from one another. The simplest things confound us.

Amber is leaving first. I fly up two days later, and Ethan joins us two days after that. I give my notice at the steel foundry and throw my scabies infested mattress in the hotel dumpster. I pack my belongings into my stolen milk crates and withdraw my life-savings of $550 from the bank. My little white Rabbit is stuffed to the ears and is ready to hop down the road.

I need to drop off my car and milk crates at my parents' house, which is four hours west in Walla Walla. From there it is another eight hours on a bus to the big airport in Seattle.

Seattle, Spokane, and Walla Walla form the tips of my Bermuda Triangle. They will suck me in and disrupt my gravity and my compass many times over the next decade.

In Spokane, I meet up with Jon. He is yet another of the lost souls that I've known since before the corps. He wants to hitch a ride to our mutual hometown, the town so nice. I can use the company. He throws his tattered travel bag in my backseat and we hit the road.

We're at mile-marker 223, halfway to our destination and two hours from anything familiar, when the police siren chirps behind me. I pull over. It's 5 am and I've been up for a few days. I don't think I'm driving straight. I know I'm not seeing straight.

"License and Registration." I give it to the officer. "How did you shatter your window?" I need to think fast. I was driving off the road about twenty miles back and I hit a reflector. It flipped up and smacked the driver's side window. I can't tell him that!

"I bought it this way."

"You, what's your name? Do you have ID?" He's looking at Jon, who nervously shifts in my passenger seat.

"Yes sir, here's my ID."

"Wait here." He returns to his car. Fifteen minutes later, another car to arrives. Now two officers approach from each side of my Rabbit.

I'm not scared of the cops. I fear what they can do to me, but not of them as people. I have a history with them. Both of my parents are cops, I got arrested in

Memphis, and I met quite a few cops in Spokane. I'm calm in these situations. It is shamefully familiar.

The officer returns on the passenger side, bends down, and looks inside. "Step out of the car please." Jon shoots me a frightened look, exits the car, and is put in handcuffs. He is arrested for an outstanding warrant.

"You too, sir," the cop says looking into my window. I exit, and he leads me to the police car. My wrist aches from the officer's firm grasp. He pushes me belly-down onto the hood, while I watch them gut my Rabbit and spill all my possessions on the side of the highway. They seize my powder-caked scale along with some other tools. They can take what they want, just let me go!

The nice man writes me a ticket for possession of paraphernalia and walks towards his car. I have made it this far, but the universe now chooses to get the police involved, just as I'm about to fly to Alaska.

I glance at the officer, not knowing what to do. "The next exit will take you to Ritzville County Jail" he offers. "Just in case you want to come get your friend."

The cops leave me to my own demise and pull away with Jon handcuffed in the back looking out like a kenneled dog. I look toward the sky to see rain clouds approaching and then look back at all my worldly possessions strewn about mile-marker 223. I seize the opportunity to pack my things better as I reload everything into my Rabbit in the rain.

"Thank you." After I paid Jon's bail, these are the only spoken words for the rest of our drive to Walla Walla.

I have about a hundred bucks and my one-way ticket to Anchorage. Is this the beginning, the end, or just a fork stuck too deep in the turkey? I feel like I am done. My slate is clean and ready to be refilled, but dark omens are making it difficult to break away. I buy the cheapest tent I can find and a bus ticket to Seattle. I have $30 left to support me in Alaska. The doors are closing and this one-way is my only way. Gravity is a bitch.

My bus from Walla Walla arrives at SeaTac airport at 7 pm but the red-eye to Anchorage doesn't leave until 3am. No money, no home, and self-exiled, I wander the airport for hours.

The faces I am remiss to examine change every 45-minutes as they board their planes and are replaced by new faces. I study their migratory habits as they go from bathroom to vending machines to countertops. I think about what exotic places they must be coming from and to where they all disappear. I envision the stories they will be able to tell.

I am a strung-out junkie on a one-way trip to nowhere, but the path through the forest has never been clearer. Survival at my northern destination will be an entirely different struggle. I don't have any real-life skills other than immortality and hand-to-hand combat. I wonder if there will be a drill instructor waiting to pick me up at the airport? I hope I won't need my combat skills when I land. Being taught how to disembowel and then having no real prospects in life seems like a dangerous thing to do to people.

Those are old demons that I now rinse from my being. My sins melt away, then replay before my eyes, in single file, marching by like the soldier I once was. Does Amber remember I'm coming to Alaska? We didn't plan our flights out of Seattle and I haven't seen her since we were all together in Spokane. She has already been in Anchorage for two days, and it's been a week since the cops emptied my car at mile-marker 223. Ethan is still in Spokane preparing to meet us in Anchorage in three days,

The moment of truth has arrived. I am on the final descent of a one-way trip, my only way to abandon ship, the conduit to my escape to the Great Northwest.

Wheels down, lights on, the flight attendant announces, "Welcome to Anchorage International Airport. It's 6:26 am local time, and the temperature outside is 46 degrees Fahrenheit. We hope you have a lovely stay in Alaska." I hope so too. I now have $12 in my pocket and a cheap tent somewhere below in the fuselage. I'm not clear how much loveliness this will provide.

The attendants usher us out of the cabin door and I am instantly hit by a chilly breeze that reminds me that I am far from home. I follow in the footsteps of those that seem to know the answers, as they lead me to the baggage claim. I gather my pack and mentally prepare about what I should do next if Amber is not here.

I see happy couples kissing, I see fathers collecting their daughters, and I see a few singles that just keep walking like they belong here. I do not. I also don't see Amber anywhere. I stand frozen. Has she forgotten? Or perhaps worse, she doesn't care that I'm here.

"You made it!" Amber sneaks up from behind me and yells into my ear. I jump and almost piss my pants. I'm not sure how I missed her. It must be difficult for Amber to be awake this early, but she still comes, and she brought her brother Stefan.

I heave my external frame pack over my shoulder, and the tent tied to the side slams into my hips. We wander outside into the brisk northern air, towards Stefan's rusty work truck.

At Amber's parent's house, I'm shown to Stefan's bunk bed. I get the top unit, but I must try to forget my childhood traumas of falling out of bunk beds.

I awaken to voices in the middle of the afternoon. The rest of the day passes in a blur until dinner time, when Amber's mother asks, "Where are you sleeping tonight?"

I am juggling an awkward fog of jetlag accompanied by the pain of withdrawals. Entering a dining room full of strangers is a challenge, but my body forces me, I have no choice, I need a good meal. I now wish I had stayed in bed.

I thought I was staying here! I surveil the room and see only stern eyes staring back at me. I must do the only thing that makes sense. I make plans to leave and with haste. I could wait until tomorrow, but I am rested now, and about to receive a hearty meal. Ethan won't be here for a few days, I'll have to figure this out on my own.

"I'm going to find a campsite!" I have a tent and sleeping bag strapped to a backpack, how hard can this be? Let's do this! I'll spend my first night in Alaska under the stars. This will be perfect.

"There's a campsite on the edge of town, we'll take you there," offers Amber. We pile into his truck and leave the awkward suburbs. I am excited, and I am eager, but that all comes crashing down when we discover that the campsite is full.

The next campground is also full, and the site after that. Amber and Stefan drive me for an hour straight south with no sign of available camping spots. It is crazy silly that we're in Alaska and I can't find a place to camp.

I'm not sure why Amber and Stefan are so resolute to following the rules and restricting me to an official campground. I'm perfectly content sleeping anywhere. I have a tent. I can't afford the rental for a site anyway. I see ample camp spots along our drive, in the wild forests, but they tell me to be careful where I pitch my tent.

"I can just camp anywhere."

"There are bears everywhere," Amber warns.

After driving for another hour, we are already halfway to Kenai, my ultimate destination. I can't expect Amber and Stefan to take me all the way, that would be just as silly as not finding a camp spot in Alaska. I will find my own place to sleep tonight.

"Please just let me out here."

Hitchhiking in Alaska is rumored to be a very safe and efficient mode of travel. This will involve trust in both the people who told me it was safe, and trust in the people who might pick me up. My choices are limited, I must test this preconception in these midnight hours. A turn-out appears on the side of the road, and we pull in. Amber is apologetic, but I am excited.

"Are you sure, are you going to be ok?" Amber asks in her most serious tone, while Stefan looks straight ahead, hands at ten and two on the steering wheel.

"Yes," I say, but I'm not overly confident in my response. Something tells me everything will be just fine, but those voices have misguided me before. I lug my pack over my shoulder and give Amber a kiss through the truck window. Amber returns the kiss and hands me an LSD tab. I wave to her brother, they turn their tail lights toward me and drive northward through the dark dusk and towering trees. I will never see them again.

I stand at the intersection of this way and that, between here, there, and wherever. The calm forest air dampens all sound. It is cold, it is dark, and I am alone.

Loose Roots

6

I emerge. I am reborn. I have paid my rite of passage. The priest gazes lovingly into my eyes and I shiver, perhaps from this cold Alaskan lake or perhaps from our locking glances. The icy waters splash from my eyes and run down my cheeks. I rise.

The congregation is still in a half-moon upon the shore. I have become numb to the cold sensation of the lake water that is freezing my demons. I have a new tribe now. I found God and like a cheap mistress, I left the bar life behind to go bear witness.

Being reborn was incredibly easy, even if uncomfortable and slightly awkward. The priest's hand remains firmly on my back, supporting my inclinations to enter the water to collect the sins I just left floating on the surface like lily pads.

The pastor's hand is trembling, stretching towards the heavens, as he shouts "Hallelujah!" He encourages me to do the same, but my forked-tongue resists. I am reborn again, tabula rasa, ready to paint on my new canvas. But still, I have complete control of my tongue. Stop it already.

Squinting into the dark recesses of the lake banks, I see no fluttering doves, no rainbows, and no Michelangelo finger of God waiting to poke me on the nose. The Apostolic Pentecostals promise me that God himself will grant me a gift like none other. I scoff, mock, and envision my neatly wrapped present attached to a child's parachute drifting down from the heavens. A simple dip in the lake is not enough to wipe out two decades of life and superstition. I will not expect miracles unless I see Excalibur, unicorns or gargoyles.

I murmur an unenthusiastic "Hallelujah?" ending the ceremony. The priest and I walk back to the shore as if we just got married and the congregation shouts congratulations as they shake my hand.

"I can take you home now," the pastor offers.

I turn to Beau. "I'll ride back with the pastor to his home so I can take a warm shower." I'm secretly waiting for God's gift to enter my blood stream. Nothing happens. The heavens still don't part, I am just cold and wet. Like a hazing or gang initiation, I am now part of the club.

The pastor lets me wear some of his size too-big jeans and Beau drives me back to my room. Beau is proud of me, I am his new spirit brother. Beau is my guide into God's kingdom, but he failed to indicate the velocity or method of arrival my gift. He drops me off at my hotel room. I open one of Bud's beers and stare at the ceiling.

For the next week, I am unable to eat. No food enters my body, only juice sustains me for these seven days. My lack of appetite is the same as when I'm hung-over or strung-out.

I work in a restaurant, I have plenty of options, but everything tastes like rubber. I try to eat eggs, but they smell foul and rancid. I attempt to eat baked chicken, this time my nose approves but my mouth can neither taste nor digest the perfect, golden-brown chicken leg. Even the mashed potatoes won't slide down my throat. Food has no place in my face or my stomach. "Well, that's a strange gift," I think to myself.

On the seventh day, my appetite returns with a fury at the exact hour that I was submerged last week. While I am enjoying my first meal as a new man, Bud happens past my table at The Glacier. We start sowing discontent at the impending winter and how we wish we could just escape its long, cold grip.

"Dude, you don't have to stay here! Why don't you go to the tropics? It's cheap and warm." said God, using Bud's mouth. We progress into drunken elaboration of Caribbean dream lands, some with endless beaches, others with timeless cultures, and all without the blanket of desperation that people feel during the Alaskan winter. There is a world outside that is prospering while we sit frozen in time.

After Jesus Christ starves me for a week, I find vibrancy in the world around me. The darkness lifts, the pine smells permeate the air, and there are more eagles gliding overhead. The tunnels of snow that lead to the supermarket melt away like yesterday's news. The long winter is also ending, the ice breaks and spring arrives on a songbird's note.

My mental stability is also returning, and my hierarchy of needs is finding its foundation of food, shelter, and security. The summer hoards aren't here yet, but Valdez is starting to prepare for its tourist season.

When Memorial Day Weekend arrives in May, so do the transients. I can then embrace the life returning to a town that has been buried in snow for five months. Summer winds are blowing in, I can come out of my cave and rummage through the forest. Expanding my circle of friends will lift me from my dark winter depression.

The days lengthen, summer is shining, and the motor homes start to fill the campgrounds. The harbor is alive with charter boats and the bay is dotted with large fishing seiners again. Across the masts of the smaller boats, I see the cannery parking. The sleeping trailers are back, parked in the exact same places they were last September. A few dread-locked fish-hippies have come into town, signaling the beginning of something familiar.

The snowline struggles to survive through the month of May, as it sneaks up the mountainside and disappears over the summit. Scurry away, snowline, your time has passed. The sun agrees and returns to its full elliptical orbit around the sky, overshadowing the moon and the aurora with dim daylight.

The summer vibrations pull me in, but the intimate understanding of what the winter can do to the spirit clarifies my timing and my fate. I won't be staying here long. I need to save enough money to escape before winter hits and I get stuck again.

God said, using Bud's mouth, "you don't have to stay here" and so I won't, but I can't go yet. I must first sweat the summer and earn my passage.

My winter friends disappear into the busy work weeks at one of the seven eating establishments. I cook from 6 am until 3 pm, but I am still left with too much extra time. A nine-hour work day, four hours of bar play, and two hours of sleep still allows me another nine hours to do as I wish. I need to find a second job.

Agility and Stability

I stand on top of Hippy Hill, looking across the water. The Alyeska Pipeline Terminal is on the opposite side looking back at me in the darkness. The terminal lights glow like a small city, illuminating the mountainside.

In 1989, an Exxon Oil Company boat was leaving the terminal when it ran aground, spilling eleven million gallons of oil into the Prince William sound, and onto the coastlines of Valdez.

The Exxon-Valdez spill was the biggest spill of its time but has unfortunately been surpassed many times. Tens of thousands of scientists, environmentalists, agencies, and good Samaritans were drawn to the area to clean up the mess.

The fish which feed the people are coated in black slime, and they also wash up dead upon the banks, along with the birds that tried to dive through the oil. Even the sea otters can't escape the wall of oil blocking the narrows that link Valdez to the ocean.

That time has passed, but the people have not forgotten. One of the oil-drenched little sea otters was named Oscar. He became an unofficial mascot of the city. After he was nursed back to health and returned to the wild, he became a symbol of triumph, hope, perseverance and illuminated the dichotomy between man and nature.

Oscar also has a restaurant named after him. It's on the city-side of the harbor, before the horse-shoe begins. It's a quick walk from anywhere, and a perfect place to look for a second job. I already know the cooks and the servers, they are part of the core.

The owner towers over six feet tall, with a powerful, muscular frame. He's in his sixties, but he could snap me in half if he wanted to. His long gray hair and his bottle-thick glasses minimize the intimidation, but his stern voice snaps me back to attention.

"Hi, I'm Al." He extends his hand.

I look at him puzzled, pause, then allow his grip to swallow my hand.

"I thought your name was Oscar?" I confess.

"Can be if you want, it's just a name." This Taoist non-answer annoys me. He does look like a large Confucius, but Al is more cynical than optimistic, more

secular than spiritual. Life has dealt him a series of blows
that ride on his shoulders like the dreams of the children
he never had. No, he's just a chill hippy who wants to surf
all day. Too bad he bought a restaurant in Alaska and
doused that dream.

Al promptly hires me at Oscar's on the Waterfront
to cook dinner. My summer rotation is to cook breakfast
and lunch at the Glacier until 2 pm. At 3 pm I need to be
at Oscar's to prep for dinner, then cook until 1 am.

I usually stop by the bar after work, until it gets
dark around 2 or 3 am. I have a few more hours to myself
before I open the Glacier for breakfast at 6 am. I don't
sleep much, but the perpetual daylight feeds me. The
blowing wind gently whispers my destiny in my ear,
reminding me to escape the winter. Life is easy when we
have a purpose, a destination, and a map to get there.

I don't have to work Thursday morning or Monday
night, I spend that time catching up on sleep and
extending my social play. The sleep cycles are a lot like
Spokane was, although here in Valdez the sun is my
chemical. It provides me with endless vigor and a
balanced reservoir of life.

My winter friends are my closest confidants, but
still more like-minds join our crew throughout the
summer. At night, we set camp fires at the beach, or play
games of pool at The Palace, but usually we bounce
between the bars. We are family, we all share the same
schedule, the strong love of life, and the lack of standard
commitments.

With the influx of the warm summer weather and motor homes, I am again kicked out of my hotel to make room for paying customers. I can keep my job this time though, so that's cool. It's also camping season, I've seen a few tents at The Hill and on the trails behind town. This is a natural progression through the seasons. I was going to move out of my room anyway, it feels too stuffy when the world is just outside.

I pitch my tent on my old concrete slab and spend half of the summer camping at Hippy Hill. It's been a lifetime since I was up here with Cole. The people aren't as friendly as I remember, and they smell a lot worse.

It's late July when Casey approaches me. "Why don't you sleep in my van? I'm not using it."

Casey works at the Palace Bar next to Oscars. Too much cocaine has given her rotten teeth, but they match her gnawing personality. She's slightly shorter than I am, about 35 years old, and shaped like a pear. She also has a deserted van parked out in a field.

I need to find a more permanent home, something between the luxury of a hotel room and the flimsiness of a cheap tent. A van would provide security and isolation, and a new feature – mobility.

"It's nothing special, but it's better than your tent and it's away from the smell of the canneries."

"Can we go there after work?" I ask.

"Yeah, of course. It's just over there," she points westward towards the edge of town. "Come by the bar when you're done closing Al's. You can drive us there." She oddly thinks I have a car. I think she is a little crazy and needs some sleep. I quickly dispel the notion that I am affluent enough to drive.

"We can walk, it's near." We do.

The van is parked in a precarious place, not just off the road but halfway into the field. The grass has grown tall around it. The blades conceal the tires and hide the rusty undercarriage. Casey's van has sat in this field through at least one winter, likely several others before. The ground is uneven, tipping the entire vehicle slightly towards its large sliding door.

Casey yanks at the side door. It slides open with a jolt that should have dislocated her shoulder. As soon as I look inside, I am instantly in love. It has a mattress! The van's interior is ripped out, exposing the oxidized metal frame. It smells like a sock puked while mating with underwear, but I have a sleeping bag to protect me.

Casey hands me the key and I sit in the captain's chair. Surprisingly, the engine sputters and then quits. After a few more times, it grumbles like a polar bear awaking from hibernation. A functioning engine is not a requirement for me though, but it's nice to know that it can be moved closer to work. For $200, this old rusty van becomes my new home. The space within these walls create the conditions for my long-term survival.

During our summer in Kenai, Colin found a little wooden shack half a mile up the street. It was barely bigger than an outhouse, but I was envious. He had space away from the noise, his own home. He called it his compartment, aptly named due to its size. I think that if he could see me now, in the comforts of my new van, he would be just as jealous now as I was then.

I now have a bedroom. My kitchen is at Al's and he has a shower there too. I no longer need to insert quarters at the Harbor Master's shower or try to sneak into the canneries to rinse away the night. I'll just park between the Palace Bar and Oscars. This new van will be the centerpiece for my newfound cosmos. I am making a new triangle with myself at the fulcrum.

My summer is spent feeding smelly workers and the wealthy-but-temporary tourists on cruise ships. I relate to the hip-fishies, but the rich tourists confuse me. How did they find their way to this magical place and only allow three hours here? They need time to explore and experience it before they get back on their ships.

The temporary tourists are much older than me, but they don't know what they are missing. I wonder if something will happen to me between now and then that will put me in their same cage with bars of haste.

The fish hippies are my people, they are me in retrospect. They have my sympathy, I know it can be grueling. The faces have changed, but their demeanors have not. This is the next class to come through this school of independence. There are a few familiar faces from last year, but mostly everyone is new.

I am salty now, I pretend to be local. My work days are still long, like the cannery days, but my destiny this summer is to put Bud's words into action, receive my gift, and be delivered to the ends of the earth.

It is a summer of revolution, full of freedom, without addictions or skeletons. The work is hard, cooking away the days, but my friends stop by the kitchen after climbing and kayaking, sharing stories of the summer opulence. My biological clock is going cuckoo with twenty hours of daylight, eighteen of them at work, but I know my body can go a week without food and almost a week without sleep.

We begin to prosper. We have gone beyond simple sustainment. We thrive, we save, and we build our own culture. We burn driftwood at the beaches and play guitar by the river. Each night after work, I have a new scavenger hunt to see who is where, which circle of friends is at the bars and who is smoking weed at Corey's house.

Summer wanes and night descends on the surrounding mountains. The sun tightens its ellipse around the sky and the days get shorter. The cannery shifts shorten to the standard ten-hours. The thick of the crowds disperse and slips at the harbor become available.

The town is no longer at maximum capacity. It's like the clouds parting, casting a shard of light to Earth prompting me to get on and go for a ride. There are a few meager weeks left to accomplish the necessary: ensuring I have both enough cash and enough summer memories to carry me forward.

My winter friends know what is coming and they are excited. They enjoy the dark, snowy months as much as they love these thriving summer scenes. I know what is coming too, but I am not like them, not at the core. I cannot plant these roots, I must find my wings and soar.

The days dwindle until it is time for departure and bid my friends farewell. I'm hitch-hiking out of here in the morning. I'll just leave this van in the field. It'd be cool if it were still here in the springtime, I could use a place to sleep when I get back. If not, that's fine too.

I'm whisking across the cloud tops, dancing like a whisper in the breeze, carried by the caw of the sea gulls on a summer reprieve. After I spend a few weeks in the triangle, I will land in Costa Rica for a new winter repentant of the dread from the last.

Eighteen months ago, I set off on my own rehab in the wilderness, prospered, then went through a deep winter depression. I snapped out of it again once the winter thawed and the sun came out. The winters have been rough, but the summers have been absolute bliss. I must find more summers. I am ready to go south.

My first stop in the triangle is to visit with friends and family to let them know I didn't get eaten by bears. I receive an icy welcome at each point along my triangle route home. My friends from Seattle, Spokane, and Walla Walla must have thought I got lost, which is almost true.

I have my own little cloud that follows me around, but I am convinced that my destiny will strike, and I will not venture into that darkness again. I do not linger. I am excited. I am alive. I've been to the edges before, but I am choosing different borders now.

I've been out of the country before too, but just to the Mexican border town of Tijuana and just for a day trip. This trip will not be as abrupt, rather I will spend the winter in the tropics waiting for the snow to melt, just as Bud suggested.

Bud's wise words permeate my destiny. They give me the drive to feel alive - I seek the light. This usually quiets the demons, but not always. I buy my escape, complete the triangle through my homeland, and fly to Central America.

The Pure Life

7

Early Ethos

I lock the door. The scenery here is shady, the bars can wait until tomorrow. I have time. There is a pit of fear bubbling in my belly. It has remnants of my first summer on the Alaskan highway, but this time the sensation is mixed with anxiety rather than desperation. My path forward is clear. I am running toward my destiny instead of away from my fate.

I've landed in Costa Rica with a pocket full of cash. This feels comfortable, but the security of cash in hand is entirely new. The tingles in my fingers stretch past my shoulders and into my soul. My energy is aglow with excitement, fear, trepidation and recklessness.
I need to sleep.

My pack slides off my back and onto the floor. The jet lag seeps away from my skin. In my room, the solitude consumes me, as I reflect on my stupidity at Spanish. The first thing I do is get out my calculator to figure out exactly how much I just spent on a taxi ride and my room. $10 for the cab ride, $17 for the room. My budget allows for $26 per day if I am to survive for the full three months. I just arrived and I'm already over budget. I'm doomed.

I fall on the bed and wake at an unknown hour. I don't have a clock and I haven't worn a watch since I was seven. I have no idea what time it was when I went to bed or what time it is now. My father's voice still echoes in my ear, "Son, get a watch!"

The construct of time is impacting my routine, my peace, further inhibiting me from fusing into the scene. I set out to beat the streets and find a time-piece. The streets are filled with locals, most of them are frantic vendors immersed in the game of hustle, the need to attain cash to survive, much like my summer scene at the restaurants, only completely different.

I stand on the corner and lean next to a pole. I see one blind man and another man with only one leg. I see some grubby guy with a microphone and a speaker tied around him like a backpack. He is whining Spanish cries for pennies through scratchy speakers and feedback. I have no pennies to give. I ate today, had a beer, bought The Tico Times and spent $40, nearly twice my allowance. Maybe it was two beers.

I thought more people would speak English here. The local flavor has overloaded my central nervous system into culture shock. Tomorrow, I'm going to find the rest of the lost gringos to help me feel at home, but today I am alone with no one to talk to.

"Gracias Bueno, Si, gracias. Bueno Bueno. Por favor? Gracias, no. Aah, si! No, no Bueno." These are the five essential words in premeditated orders that one must know to pretend you understand anything you are being told. I can parrot these phrases convincingly, but I'm painfully aware that I don't understand anything that people are saying to me. I can fake it, but this creates problems when I'm asking for directions. I often walk in circles, but at least my dignity is intact.

I met a new friend today, Edwin. He's local and he's broke. It's funny the people I meet. As we walk the streets, Edwin just hangs around, making conversation, while I run errands and finally find a clock.

I smoked my first Cuban cigar today. It tasted just like – wait for it - a cigar. There is too much hype surrounding this thing. I tore it apart and made ten little cigars and shared with Edwin.

We part ways for the day but make plans to meet again at 11 am, since I can now tell the time. I arrive home with a square, pink alarm clock with dead hands. Stupid thing is broken. I guess I got the discounted non-functional version. I'm just not meant to know the time. I wake at 11:30 am. Sorry Señor Edwin, I will probably never see you again.

Week Three

Is today Friday? I do not know. I need a calendar, just a small one. I may have given up on the watch and clock, but perhaps I need to measure time in days and weeks instead. Today is calmer, cooler, and I am focused on my future, but it would be ideal to understand my starting time.

I need to find a new place. The Tico Times has a listing for a studio apartment behind La Universidad (that's means 'university' in Spanish, not 'the universe's dad'). The way I figure it, more people will speak English around the school than people in the San Jose slums.

I must explore and bear witness, but I'm timid of the busses. My brain tells my mind, "We can just walk the seven kilometers with a full pack, we have all day. This will save $10." After one short kilometer, I listen to my body instead, and hail a taxi to check out an apartment behind the university.

I sign a month-long lease for $150. My new apartado is in a modern building, complete with a security gate and a pretty Chinese owner, whom I will never see again after I pay rent. Aside from a bed, the room is barren, much like my lust for the owner. The studio is painted in that blinding hospital white, an appropriate blank canvas to rival my tabula rasa.

I now have a home. It shields me from the evils of the world. It is much bigger than my van back in Alaska, parked in a field, currently caving under the weight of snow. I paid one month's rent but intend to be out exploring the jungles and beaches long before the following month's rent is due.

Ironically, this is my first real apartment anywhere, and I'm probably going to desert it like a cheap one-night stand. That would be a pleasant addition, a night stand - just one - next to the lonely bed.

Yesterday I walked the wrong way and ventured away from the populated areas, arriving at some cheap local housing units. Some dirty little schoolgirl on a bike started pointing fingers at me and laughing. I guess I need a better map, perhaps also a dictionary that can translate little girl's laughs. I am a cow in a herd of sheep, a big, black and white spotted Brahma bull. I'm a traitor to my own wishes and this little girl senses this.

I've been searching for Spanish schools, camping spots, girlfriends, and occasionally I'll covet an alarm clock I see in a window of a shop. I haven't had any luck with the girlfriend, I can't camp in the city, and the cosmos says I'm not worthy of a time-piece. I'm spinning in circles, but it's only been three weeks.

I have had considerably more success in the hunt for a Spanish school. I enrolled in a class that starts on Monday. Small class size, friendly environs, and energetic travelers. This is what beckons me.

There are six other class rooms with a few students in each. The common areas buzz with energy and excitement during the breaks. The school also organizes activities like Merengue and Salsa dance lessons, rafting trips, and trips to the volcanos - or anywhere else our wings may wish to flutter. Let's see where this wind blows.

Week Four | *Plummeting*

I want to jump off a bridge, like a real bridge. My adrenaline bucket is empty, my soul needs nourishment, I need a shot. I'm going bungee jumping!

The bridge is only two hours north and we arrive at a muggy 10 am. It is God's day, Sunday, I hope I don't meet him today. My nervous energy and butterfly excitement turn to dread as we arrive and park the van.

We exit the van and step upon the bridge. Like a plank over shark infested waters, the Puente Rio Colorado overlooks the pristine green jungle. It provides passage over the thin sliver of a river, while threading these two mountainsides together. I can barely see the river below, and as I look over the edge, I get sensations of vertigo.

"Ochenta metros," my guide says. I get out my calculator. It says "262 feet." Oh my, no.

As we stand, looking in awe, a young man in a harness walks towards us. I pay him $20 and step onto his scale. The guide writes my weight in black permeant ink on the backs of my hands.

There is a group of spectators with cameras on the other side of the platform. I think they are reporters ready to film my death. I am the third one to jump, which provides me with ample time to contemplate my choices and my love of God. I throw a rock over the edge of the bridge and lose sight before it hits the bottom.

It is my turn. The guide instructs me to step into a standard climbing harness as he wrenches it around my crotch. Next, he straps the bungee to my calves. He shows me two smaller bungees that join up with the long bungee attached to the bridge. I inspect them, and I realize they will be secured around my legs by six-inches of Velcro. I was thinking buckles, maybe a chain, or some special boots, but I guess this will do. He shackles the cords to my calves and motions me to the ledge, where I will leap into the nether.

As I walk closer to the platform, the operator makes a loop with a cord and drapes it over my arm. This is just like my father did with the garden hose back on the farm. Much like my farm chores, I will be responsible to tend my own tools. With each successive loop, I inch closer until I step upon the platform.

I look down, my head gets woozy, and I teeter. It's a long way down, I wonder if that rock has hit the bottom yet. The operator put his hand on my shoulder. I look away from the depths and find his eyes fixated on mine. "Ready?"

I look around at the crowd and scan their eyes. I smile back, then look at the man and say "Vamos! Deseame Suerte!" I can use all the luck they can wish upon me.

The crowd counts down, "Tres, dos, uno, SALTA!"

I bend my knees and leap out as far as I can. This is admittedly a pathetic jump, since my feet are hobbled together and this cord is draped over my arm. I envisioned an elegant swan dive, but I'm just happy I cleared the platform.

All that exists are the winds, the peace of the free fall, the scenic rocks, and the bright green trees that are quickly getting closer. Then I rebound, rise, and float, before I descend again towards the trees that look like little shrubs below.

In this wink of time, between rising and falling, I am free from the tension of both the bungee and of the world. Unlike the path that has brought me here, now I float effortlessly. The path before me now is scripted by gravity. I'm just here for the ride.

The cycle ends and my heart beats strong. I hear it in my head. My thoughts are clear, and my senses heightened. My blood is coursing, my aura is glowing, I FEEL ALIVE!

I close my eyes and breathe in the exhilaration. All is quiet, except for a light breeze whispering in my hair. I look up to see the bridge and the bungee that is my lifeline. Then I turn my head and look down. There is a sliver of a river below, but should this cord snap, I would hit the massive boulder directly beneath me.

Instantly, the euphoria is sucked from my gut and my survival instincts are thrown into distress. I am suspended midair, hanging by my feet with Velcro. My heart is racing, but I calm myself. This is not the right place for a panic attack. I am stuck halfway between the safety of the ledge from where I jumped, and a plummet that would end it all. My life is suspended.

I see the upside-down outlines of the men up on the platform. They are lowering a small rope and guiding it towards me with long shepherd's hooks. While I hang like a cocoon dangling from a branch, I grab that rope and lock it onto my harness. This rope ignites the catalyst that frees me from this suspended state.

I sit on my harness, perched like a scared songbird, waiting for the men above to pull me back to the ledge. The blood flows from my head back to my feet. I look upward and see the ledge from where I jumped only a few minutes ago, before I went through a rabbit hole.

I look around in comfortable accomplishment. The rush of the jump, my heart beat while hanging, this feeling is fading, but the day is not done. There's a huge festival in the mountains about twenty kilometers north. We arrive at the festival and walk as far as the Red Cross medical tent. We move some tables aside and collapse in the grass. We don't need medical attention, we need unabated space.

The price of going up – is coming down. The adrenalin dump is strong, but we are now bonded through our plummets. There are a few thousand people here, all speckled across the grass and between the trees. I sip my Bavaria beer, eat a coleslaw taco, and sit back to absorb the distant beat of a drum.

Ribbons in the Wind

8

Week Six | Settled and Comfortable

Back at school, a new batch of students arrive from around the world. The community is growing. My classmates are from Johannesburg, and they speak English with what sounds like an Australian accent. The guy looks Australian too, I think he's lying. His name is Demarco and his girlfriend is Cara.

Her name, *Cara*, means *face* in Spanish. "Hey, Face, what are you doing tonight?" Face and Demarco are my new favorite people. She laughs when I call her Face to her face. They both like to laugh, they laugh all the time. They also like to watch English movies dubbed in Spanish, then with English subtitles turned on. It feels counter-productive.

There are three other people in my class, but my focus is fixed only upon Tanja from Germany. She has translucent blue eyes and a piercing smile. Her long golden hair lays flat upon the side of her face, next to her dimply cheeks. Her eyes look like the ocean and her skin the sand, with curves like the windblown dunes.

Over the next few weeks, we grow close through a series of school sponsored events. We dance salsa and merengue, but despite my lessons, I still dance like I am just rhythmically standing, weaving to the beat. I grew up in mosh pits, not on ballroom floors. Tanja thinks it's cute. We enjoy culture talks and trips to the zoo. We wander around the plaza looking at shops. We volunteer to cook for the big school party. My isolation melts away. I belong.

I haven't left San José yet, not really. My heart is pulling me away from the bustle of the city, towards quieter scenes, sandy beaches, and flowing waves. I want to frolic in the forest and gallop in sea mist that is ejected by ocean currents. I want to hike to exotic waterfalls, find monkeys, and chase lizards. I want to see the country.

Tanja and I both graduate from our Spanish classes on Friday, and I use 'graduate' as an expression of not having enough time or money to continue. We make plans to go to the beach in Puerto Viejo in three days.

After I hit rock bottom, I slowly crawled out from my deep pit of despair. On the way up from my spiral, I found little sparkles that glisten like the fish looking up through the sea. These shiny sparkles glow in the night and illuminate the path. They are the pieces of hope and moments that we cling to during dire times. They give me life, and they are everywhere if we just look. Tanja sees them too and points out the ones that I miss.

We are partners, each anxious for the weekend's tranquility. When school is out tomorrow, she'll gather her things and we'll meet at my Apto to start our adventure together.

As our final class is dismissed, Tanja talks to another Swiss couple. We are all students, we are friendly. I like these guys. I don't speak German, but I think Tanja just invited them to come on our romantic escape on the Caribbean coast. That is not how I saw this weekend going, I want to be alone with Tanja.

We arrive in Puerto Viejo late in the evening to the smells of tuna kabobs and fresh roasted vegetables. The buildings are thatched but strong, with a few brick buildings scattered throughout. A hurricane or the big bad wolf could do some serious damage here. The painted walls have faded, and the Caribbean pastel colors have blended into the woodwork.

Our rooms are shabby little wooden spaces with planks for shutters. The Swiss are in one, while Tanja and I share another. The rooms have mattresses and we have sleeping bags, that's all we need. A mosquito net hangs from the ceiling, shrouding the mattress.

I always thought these were just for princesses. I whisk it aside, exposing the mattress to the elements.

Tanja scolds me, "No, leave that, it's for bugs!" She throws her sleeping bag inside and lays down. I pull the net over her, put my hand on her hip for a moment and let her know I'm going to sit on the porch and write.

While Tanja is inside worrying about bugs, I sit on the veranda looking out into the dark jungle, wondering what beasts rattle in the trees. I fear malaria and dengue. I fear a monkey coming over and throwing dung at me. I fear the fer de lance snake climbing up from the shadows, as I sit unprotected surrounded by wet lushness. My hip knife is unsheathed, lying on the table next to my pencil, my water, and my headlamp. I fear what might jump up from the bushes and bite my cock as I walk to the edge and take a piss on the foliage.

My hopes of a romantic getaway bubble and fizzle, while my sense of adventure prospers. We roll around on the black sand beaches, snorkel the corrals, and look for monkeys. We ride horses on the beach and through the jungles, returning them wet to the stables.

The nights are spent dancing in the sand to live reggae and calypso. With our sandals in one hand and our other hands holding, we migrate between the huts and follow the sounds down the beaches. Mono Locos, Coco Locos, passion fruit martinis - all the drinks are made with fresh and exotic fruits that tickle our taste buds.

It's Tuesday now, and we've been on the beach for four days. The ocean and the village are pure, which makes my heart burst. Maybe I'm just tired, heartbroken, and sunburnt. We talk about where we should go next, but I remain neutral and numb. Tanja is set on going to Quepos, on the western, Pacific side of the country.

I need to let Tanja go there alone, and I need to go my own way. I should have bought her that rose in the plaza. Free as a bird, migratory, this is the dream of my life story. One that I will again betray.

I'm going north, and Tanja is going west with the Suizas. I have been completely engrossed, yet never getting any closer than to her than to smell her hair and gaze into her eyes. The girl of my dreams has different dreams, and I have awoken into yet another fantasy. I think I'll throw this wish back and catch another.

Repetition beats at my skull like raindrops in a downpour. "Go. Go. Go." I cannot stay, I must go away. My desire for autonomy mandates my motions. My imagination is flush with exotic imagery of volcanoes and hot springs, jungles and beaches.

I'm halfway through my time here and I still have $1,600. That's enough for quite a few bus tickets, but I'm not sure about food and rooms. I have all my camping gear, I'm flexible. Let's see where these roads lead.

Costa Rica is tiny by the standards of most countries. In just one day, I can bus from the Pacific Ocean to the Caribbean Sea, east to west across the country. Two days in a bus can take you from the north to south. These are the crosses I make, driving to the four corners of the compass.

I can't become too disconnected, I might snap the tether that ties me to San Jose. Like the hands of a clock, my radius is outlined and it does not include crossing international borders. Even vagabonds have boundaries.

Week Eight | Hybrid Homes

When I was in Walla Walla two months ago, I met up with one of my dearest friends, Jazmin. We've been friends since we were ten. She is a constant from the hometown triangle, a tree with shared roots. When I saw her two months ago, in the weirdest flash of coincidence, Jazmin tells me "I'm going to Costa Rica in the spring!"

Spring is fast approaching, and I need to contact Jazmin. It costs 10,000 colones in coins to call Seattle and I don't have that kind of energy. At every opportunity, I call collect to the same phone number I've had for years.

No one ever picks up, so I continue to forge new relationships. I cannot pause for uncertainties. Either she doesn't want to accept my collect charges from Central America, or the number I have is obsolete.

Is she still coming? What day is she coming? What are her destinations? Does she expect me to meet her in San Jose? Although it's a complicated route to get back to San Jose, it only lasts about five hours.

I've been on the Pacific coast for ten days, camping in the isolated paradise town of Montezuma. I took a bus, a boat, and another bus to get here, so I've been hesitant to leave after all this trouble. It may also be true that I am ensnared by the lullaby of ocean waves and fruit drinks. The days are blending into weeks and the calendar is irrelevant. Plans are fickle. I like it here, but Jazmin would never find me.

My tent is perched right by Amy and Wendy whom I met at the bar when I first got here. Amy is cute and smart. She just graduated college last June, but she is already a writer and assistant editor for an outdoor sporting magazine. I have just washed the Marines away and got clean from addictions. We're coming from different ends of different spectrums, but we connect.

Wendy is pretty, but I like Amy better. College girls are trouble for vagabonds, I may end up evicting myself from Montezuma like I just did in Puerto Viejo with Tanja.

Amy is a small-framed, small-town girl from Toledo, Ohio. She's doing the same thing I am. We're out to see the world and get away from home, but she brought a friend along for her journey. I am alone.

Amy and I are coming from different directions, but our paths have converged, miles from home, and miles from our pasts. We are equals, camping on the beach and relishing in freedom.

The first and most common question people lead with is "Where are you from?" This is sometimes awkward for me, I'm not sure what kind of images a town called Walla Walla conjures in people's minds. I tell her anyway.

"Really, Walla Walla?" Amy quickly asks. "Do you know Ty Thompson?"

I'm shocked. Ty is core to my youth. "Why yes, I do! How do you... why do you... that's weird!"

"I worked with him at Yellowstone National Park in Wyoming last summer!" She says this with an excitement equal to my surprise, as we form an instant bond through matched history and connections.

This country now has two distinct lines to people I've known since I was twelve. Jazmin may be coming to Costa Rica, and now I learn that Amy knows my good friend Ty! The boundaries of my world have just pushed out and gotten a little bit bigger.

I sit with Amy at the top of one of only two freshwater waterfalls in the world that flow directly into the ocean. It's a thing of beauty. Start at the door to my tent, turn left, walk for two hours along Playa Cocolito, the little coconut beach, and arrive at the waterfall. This place combines a tranquil hike along the beach with freshwater swimming amidst the glory of flowing nature.

We hike to other waterfalls around the area, usually coming back into town around 5 pm for dinner. This is also the same time the bus arrives from San Jose every day. After today's hike, I see the bus, and then my eyes attempt to deceive me.

Tanja is sitting on a pile of six backpacks on the sidewalk in front of my favorite café. It seems that Tanja is trying to make this difficult for me. Montezuma is my escape, my sanctuary away to mend my emotions. My fight or flight instincts start to tingle as my emotions and frustrations surge.

Tanja is sitting with Taylor, one of the other travelers from school. We never got along, mostly because Tanja liked me better. It seems the opposite is true now. Taylor is also in a very bad mood, that makes me smile. It's probably nothing though, I know they had an unusual route of travel to get here. I did that route last week.

Amy is at my side when I approach Tanja and Taylor. "Como estan!" I am gleeful, ignoring the jumble of emotions that simmers under the surface, but still genuinely happy to see Tanja's dimples.

We recount the days that have passed since we last saw each other. Tanja has new life emanating from her accent. She is energized, but Taylor looks exhausted. I am confused, but I won't be phased from my path. The wind is strong. "Where can we pitch our tents?" Tanja asks.

I pause. The last thing I want is six new tents around my shady little campsite paradise, nestled in the obscurity of droopy palm trees and the ocean breeze. My tent is only one naked hop in the night away from Amy's tent. These two little microcosms from two different lives that I've already lived in Costa Rica are converging here in Montezuma. The country feels a little bit smaller now.

I don't lie to Tonja. "There's no room for that many people to camp unless you want to pitch your tents in the sun. You'll have to wake up at 8 am every day, the heat will drive you out of your tent." I look at Taylor and smile.

"We'll just check into a hostel," Tanja says, looking at Taylor and smiling. Touché, my girl, touché.

"Is there anywhere to go dancing?" This is the first time that Taylor has spoken since we saw each other. We're having a beach fire tonight, but I don't really want them to come with Amy and me. I would rather they disappear into the nether. I'm in a new place.

"Yes, I know some places you can go dancing!" I give them instructions to the furthest one I know.

Week Nine | The Cloud Forest

I think God's tongue once licked this entire land, leaving behind divine slobber from coast to coast. We've escaped the sandy beaches and palm trees, now we enter the lush green forests on the edge of another pristine national park. The three of us - Amy, Wendy, and I - are doing a 3-day hike through the MonteVerde Cloud Forest Reserve. That's the plan, anyway.

My pack weighs fifty pounds, and has thin, slicing shoulder straps. I'm carrying jeans, combat boots, camping gear, and a pair of horrendous binoculars. I am not very agile. I also wish I didn't smoke so much. This thought makes me light a cigarette.

The first day is a rugged, rolling five kilometers, mostly dense and steep. Naturally, we get lost and add four kilometers to our first day, but the sign was pointing in the wrong direction. We are not dissuaded. The climate is temperate, while the company and moods are pleasant.

The trail is always going either up or down, only flattening briefly before the next hill. We cross suspension bridges spanning streams, obscured by the dense foliage below. A six-foot cloud racer snake slithers across a huge boulder and reminds me to watch carefully where I step, and which vines I grab. It reminds me of a movie I once saw where the natives pop out on the other side of the bridge with spears and arrows. The jungle is hypnotic and meditative. My mind has traveled even further than our feet have carried us today. We arrive at the first shelter.

We drop our packs, and watch the sky darken. A troupe of howler monkeys rustle in the trees and we chase after them. They easily escape. A bioluminescent headlight beetle flies between the vines stretched across our paths. We end our night chase, return to the shelter, and abruptly put our heads down for a deep sleep.

Day two starts with a torrential downpour. Our muscles are still tired from yesterday's climbs, but the rain today has amplified my lack of proper gear. My attire is entirely inappropriate. This gear worked well in the Marines, in the hot and dry California climate. Here in the muck of Central America, I should have brought my jungle boots and packed more useful weight.

I have one poncho. It's big enough for either me or my pack, but not both. To keep all my other clothes dry, I must sacrifice what I am wearing, along with any semblance of comfort, so that I might be dry tomorrow, also betting that the rain will subside.

My combat boots are caked with mud and slipping on every surface. I have mud in every crevice. My jeans are like wet clay and god is sculpting me into his masterpiece. My socks are disintegrated. They scurried away to the front of my boots, as if they fear my heels.

The day passes in misery, until we exit the thick of the jungle. The mist parts and like a mirage of a castle in the sky, we see the left-over Quaker shelter where we will sleep tonight.

At the gates of the refuge, we are greeted by a working party of four Ticos, a Canadian, and a guy from

Michigan. They are here to study the white-nosed coati and look for jaguars. I find a sharp stick to scrape and squeeze the mud from my jeans, while the Canadian plays renditions of James Taylor on his guitar.

The rain offers a metronome of pitter-patter against the rustic steel shelter. The water-powered generator doesn't work, but I like the candles. We don't need electric light. The flickering on the walls create a serenity in the most hectic of atmospheres. Everything becomes calm while nature rages outside. I need a candle inside my head.

It is the third day, and today we will complete the circle back to the beginning. My pack is even heavier, with the weight of wet clothes, but we have grown accustomed to this fog-soaked forest. The drenched green grass, fading through different shades of lush, draw us into the wonder of the moment. In this place, the perpetual wetness births mud until the trees fall from the sludge.

The rain fizzles after the first few hours, the sun peaks through the trees, and the road flattens out. The remaining kilometers turn into manicured trails, heading back to the park gate and the entrance station. We pass a middle-aged couple that stops to stare at us. We pay little attention and hike past them. We must look like we just crawled out of the middle of the earth. We are out of the park by 4 pm, take a taxi to a hotel, and re-enter the civility of the tiny village.

Worlds Collide

9

J azmin is an endearing friend from my youth, core to the crew, who is coincidentally coming to Costa Rica while I am here. I call her from the hotel as I've done relentlessly for weeks, but this time she answers!

"Can you meet me at the airport at 8:30 am on Wednesday? I'll be there in two days!" Excitement permeates her voice. I must answer now, we won't speak again before she leaves Seattle and arrives here.

"Sure!" I say, without much consideration.

My current plan is to relax with Amy in the hot springs at Arenal Volcano and melt our muscle tensions away. Our long hike through MonteVerde has ended and Amy, Wendy, and I are looking for the next thrill.

Amy is my Costa Rica now, we spend every waking moment together, but the next path is clear, I will again disappear, to pursue this deeper loyalty with Jazmin. Amy and I are destined to end eventually, we both know this. The inevitability is undeniable, but we haven't spoken of it. We have not spoken of much lately. She became distant during that long hike. A clear sign.

"I have a friend coming in from Seattle that arrives on Friday." My tone matches my perplexed face. "I need to get her at the airport," I tell Amy. I'm not sure if I need to explain, but I am sincere, and the air is clear. I continue. "I'll meet you in Arenal the day after tomorrow, after I get Jazmin!"

That was six days ago. A new phase is beginning to emerge from all the little seeds I've planted throughout my life. Those seeds are sprouting, and their roots are tangling with the winds. It's impossible to know which way they will grow.

Week Ten | Detoured

I only intended to spend one night in San Jose, just one, then go to the airport, get Jazmin, and head back to the hot springs. Night fell on San Jose, and I went for a stroll to the bar.

"Hello, miss, do you speak English?" I pose the question to a slender blonde lady walking alone in front of the cathedral.

"Yes!" She replies, startled, in a familiar German accent.

"Do you know where the Beatle Bar is?"

"No," she says, "Do you know where Las Rosas is?" We're both looking for different bars, but neither of us can find what we are looking for. Fate is quirky.

"I'm Daniella, from Germany." Her accent is familiar. It reminds me of Tanja. I like it. Daniella doesn't have Tanja's dimples, but she has her spirit. She is bold, with a poise and posture that emanate confidence. She's five years older than I am, nearly thirty, but out here on the road these little things don't matter. Her butterscotch hair is pulled back into a pony tail that drips down her spine like honey. It billows like the ribbons on her dress. She has eyes of stained church glass and a character cuter than bunnies.

We find a classy reggae joint and dance towards the dawn until the lights come on. I walk her to her hotel. At the door, we share an embrace, face to face, our tongues entangle.

"Meet tomorrow for Breakfast?" She asks.

"Yes, breakfast, I'll call you!" I am looking for something more immediate, but it is time to go. I walk away, and realize I never told her about Jazmin coming tomorrow. I don't owe anything to anyone. Although the optics are obscure, this is the beginning of a beautiful change of current.

I wake up at 10:30 am with my eyelids glued to my eyes. Jazmin arrived two hours ago and I'm still in bed! I rise to shower and revel in my state of indecision. I defer breakfast with Daniella, I know where she lives, I can go there later. Right now, I need to find Jazmin!

The taxi drops me off at the airport. Jazmin is nowhere to be found. Coming into San Jose derailed my plans to go to Arenal Hot Springs, but I did tell Jazmin I might be there if I don't make it to the airport.

In a rare flash of clarity, I realize she may try to go straight to the hot springs to find me. I check my guidebook and head to the bus station, it leaves in an hour! It's a long shot, but worth pursuing. Otherwise we may never connect in this country.

My taxi pulls into Central Station and the first sight I see is a frightened Jazmin sitting atop of her pack waiting for the bus. "Jazzy, you're here!" I proclaim in utter surprise.

"I waited at the airport for two hours. Then I tried calling your hotel, but no one answered," she states sadly. My heart sinks, my selfish activities last night nearly left my dear friend wandering aimlessly about in a foreign country. I exaggerate my worth.

"I had an interesting night last night which led me to oversleep. But we're here now!" We exchange hugs and kisses and rejoice at finding each other in this bustling city in Central America. The cosmos has united us.

There's no hurry to get to the volcano now. I turn to Jazmin, "Let's get you checked into my room and drop off your pack." She makes small talk about the flight, but she is still bitter that I made her find her own way from the airport to the bus station. Now I must compound my ignorance. "I need to go pick up my new friend at her hotel and we can all have some lunch. Sound like a plan?" I query Jazmin, fully anticipating friction.

"Yeah, let's do it!" She is ready to settle into the city after the flight, waiting at the airport, then finding her own route to the correct bus station. It's the same indoctrination I had when I arrived. I don't feel too guilty.

Its noon when we get to Daniella's hotel and she is still asleep in her room. "I'll be down in 5-10 minutes," she says through the intercom at the gate. My heart is pounding. I sit on the curb with Jaz thinking about the predicament I have created. It's unwise to bring a female friend on a second date.

Daniella comes down from her room. She looks at me, then at Jazmin. I break the ice, "Hey, I have a friend here. She just arrived from Seattle." I introduce Jazmin to Daniella.

"Ok, let's all go eat then," she says with a cheery smile that would humble Mona Lisa. My heart slows, my aura explodes, and I realize that I need to stop worrying about other people.

We leisurely walk around the plaza, letting the day trickle away. I get to know Daniella, Daniella gets to know Jaz, and Jaz gets to know San Jose. We see the city, drink Mora juice, and start a beautiful twist. While collecting these two new travel partners, I've resigned to the fact that I will never see Amy and Wendy again, unless we have another Tanja coincidence, or a Ty coincidence. I'm not sure what would happen if I tried to travel with Amy and Wendy, with still partnering with a friend from home and my new fling I met last night. No, I'm taking Jazmin and Daniella to the Caribbean coast instead.

Week Eleven | *Second Paradise*

We hop on a five-hour bus out of San Jose, bound for Puerto Viejo. This is the same place where Tanja and I had our first non-romantic escape with the Swiss couple. That time was merely a weekend introduction. This time, my second time, I feel local. I've been here before, but now I am with a new crew of three.

Upon on our arrival on the Caribbean coast, we greet the locals and chat about the weather. "It's a gonna pour, the I-Man say." The locals warn us in their Jamaican accents to stay away this weekend or get drenched.

The wet season is here, and the torrents of rain are draining the positive vibes. I and I agree, but we are three banshees, peaceful and free. We spend the week in wet luxury, swinging in hammocks. The rain inhibits most activities, except for ganja, alcohol, dancing, and admiration of beauty, both biological and earthly.

Our cabin is a paradise next to the water, with a red hammock hovering on our open-air verandah. The coconuts and palm trees cloak us from prying eyes. The water slaps the rocks below at high tide in the twilight.

The clouds are discouraging, yet do not diminish the quality of our serenity. The moonlight has arrived, providing a soft glow on the verandah. Sensing the dusk, the ocean's reflection provides a visual path leading to the beach. The branches of neighboring palms hang next to my balcony, reaching out to protect me from an unwanted fall from this absolute peace.

The hammock gives Jazmin a big hug while the palms cradle me. The cool breeze keeps the humidity from sweating my chilled Imperial beer. The second coming has gone, and we've made it past Peter.

The children play outside our billowing curtain at Playa Negra. I see a little girl playing on the black sand beach, covering herself from head to toe, blending in with her environment. I startle her as I jog past. I wave to her mother and she waves back. I bend down, pick up some black sand, and rub it on my face too. She giggles.

"Stills a gonna rain," Ja Man Rasta say. People here walk slow and leave their shops unattended to offer a good morning word of peace to anyone who will listen. The thick green and red stripes of Jamaican influence adorn the buildings. Rumors of crime plague the travel books, but the Ja man say "No trouble ay're. You is safe."

Since time began, rocks turn to sand
through pressure, wind, and water.
She's a timeless beauty without duty,
so calm, tranquil, and proper.

The village wills what the people want,
without a stop for cause.
Diving, fishing, surfing, swimming –
the list goes on and on.

From dawn till dusk, the playa must
hold home to everyone.
From dusk till dawn, the night comes on,
and the village dances with lust.

The maidens fair, with their long dark hair,
stretching towards the Earth,
I have dreamed of scenes like these
ever since my Birth.

Rocky ocean, crashing waves,
against a sand so strained.
Ancient therapy foretells a history
of a pure life yet plain.

Paradise waters and the star filled sky,
on the horizon we watch and fly,
above the mountains so clearly rugged,
as the moon slowly trots by.

Riptides

10

The roads are softly coming to an end again. Jazmin has gone to meet some other friends from home that were also coming to Costa Rica. I knew I overestimated my worth. Daniella is also going to Germany after the weekend and I am flying home in seven days.

Daniella and I need to plan our farewell weekend, just the two of us. We can go north to see turtles, or maybe head south to Nicaragua. We can even go to Montezuma. I'm sure my other two girlfriends, Amy and Tanja, have since left that town.

We sit passively on the porch looking out at the ocean and listening to the waves. My feet are on the railing causing my shorts to slide down and reveal my tan lines. Daniela is behind me busily preparing for the evening. Go girl go. Whatever you decide is fine with me.

We awake at 7 am to catch the bus. We plan to sleep at Playa del Coco, but first we must go through Tiliran, and then Liberia. It took six hours to get to the beach, and we quickly discover that the place is extremely boring. It does not match our energies. We stay only long enough to finish our passion fruit smoothies and catch another bus to anywhere else.

After three more buses and a man in a Mercedes, we arrive in Tamarindo on the Pacific side. We just diagonally crossed the country in one day trying to find a place to sleep tonight. Time is irrelevant, but the end of the escapade draws near.

The tiny waves break twenty feet from the shore and travel in a slow ripple back out to sea. The bubbles look like they are going the wrong way on an escalator, aliased in place. The dark comes, the ocean disappears, but the seawater air still permeates our remaining senses. We saunter around town for the rest of the evening.

Night blends into the day. We awake to the creaky fisherman chattering below on their way to fish for Marlin. I pull back the dusty curtains to reveal a small sun-soaked city overlooking the sea. The ocean casts its punches at the rocks at high tide and at low, breathing in, then out so slow.

The push-pull of the tides, the yin-yang of the ecosystem, they illustrate the procession of life as our earth breathes the wind. Ebb, flow, wane, in, out again- it mimics the cycle of all things that exist.

After a few hours in one of the tide pools, Daniella goes back to the room to change. I stay behind to float in the ocean some more. I lay my things on the bank and wade into the waves. I float on my back in the calm water, looking skyward. The waves lull me into my dream state.

I drift hypnotically watching the clouds until a brisk wave snaps me back to the present. The waves are choppy. They are starting to thrash me around. I abandon my perfect views of the clouds above and begin to tread water, trying to see the coastline.

The waves no longer run in a straight line to and from the beach like the bubbles on the escalator. They are now coming at me from all sides. Left, right, forward, back. My orientation is twisted. I cannot see where I started. I have been caught in a riptide and nearly swept out to sea.

My muscles tighten and panic grips my core. I do not know how far I've drifted from the beach or which way to get back. I must find my way back to shore, or I shall surely perish.

As I learn the rhythm of the waves, I ride the crests. They thrust me above the surface of the water, but quickly disappear and again obscure me in the choppy waves. I ride the peaks in circles like a rodeo bull, trying to find my way out of the arena and back to the sand.

I glimpse a thin sliver along the horizon, nearly gone from view. I take note of the sun's position in the sky, so I don't get turned around again. I confirm my orientation and swim directly towards the sliver of land I saw. My shoes are over there somewhere.

I've exhausted all the energy in my arms and the sliver of land is no closer. I am alarmed again, not for fear of being lost, but this time for fear of being too weak to stay afloat. I tread water and eventually return to my former skyward gaze floating on my back to allow my muscles to rest and to reflect on my fear of drowning.

I read a passage in my guidebook a few weeks ago when I was researching Tamarindo. It stated that "if caught in a riptide, swim in diagonals back to the shoreline." That's silly, I thought. Everyone knows the quickest route between two points is a straight line. This defies convention.

A riptide is a tidal jet, a tunnel of water with a strong current that carries everything right out to sea, ignoring the pulse of the tides. The moon's pull of the oceans does not impact riptides the same as standard currents. They go straight out to sea underneath the surface waves. They are caused by fast-flowing estuaries that bring the silt out to the sea.

My day pack, my beach towel, and my future are all sitting on the banks of just such an estuary. The silent force of the riptide is slowly separating me and the bank.

As I lay here floating on my back, thinking about this concept, I also wonder what I have to lose. I tried it my way. I must try something new, I'll swim in zig-zags. My arms feel waterlogged again after exhausting all my energy on the first few spurts. My mind travels back to the Marines, and the training, digging deep to find the will to fight. I flip that switch.

I analyze the waves and see more glimpses of land. On my back, I kick until I need to rest. I bob around to make sure I'm zigging and zagging in the right directions, then kick a while longer. Rest. Kick. Rest. Rest. Kick.

My legs have considerably more endurance than my arms, but all my limbs are now depleted. My arms are dead. They feel like my hands did after the first day of set-netting on Jim's boat. They are limp and impotent. My legs are my only salvation back to shore.

I bob again. It looks like the shore might be getting closer. My eyes sting from saltwater, do they deceive me? I see blurry shapes dotting the horizon. They look like huts or maybe shops. Is that even my original beach?

There is no lifeguard, but he wouldn't be able to see me anyway, I am still too far out. A lifeguard would be useless in this situation unless he saw me float away an hour ago. I have drifted out to sea and am now crawling my way back. Rest. Kick. Rest.

The shore is so close I can sense it, but my arms and legs can no longer tread water. I feel like quitting, and letting my body sink to the bottom. The time of rest between my kicks has increased from seconds to minutes. I lie here skyward, just as I was doing before I was interrupted by choppy waves.

The fear of sharks or jellyfish never enters my mind. There are more pressing matters that are guaranteed to exist. I don't have the energy to wonder what else might happen. I am ignorant about other risks in the abyss until something tickles my toe. It is pleasant. It is familiar. It. Is. SAND!

The beach has risen to meet me, to congratulate me on my safe return. I don't have the energy to turn around and look at the beach, but I know it is there, right behind me, sweet land. I kick at the ground, while each successive wave pushes me a little further up the beach.

I just learned what it feels like to be a dead body washing ashore. My arms are limp, my legs are spent, my core is stretched, my face is sunburnt - but I am on land.

As I lay here, arms outstretched like Christ, a face appears directly over mine, blocking the sunlight. "Are you okay?" Daniella looks worried.

Two hours have passed since I last touched land. The tide has risen considerably and is about to snatch my bag. I wonder - if the sea had swallowed both me and my bag, would the officials deny my existence when my mom calls the Embassy? Only Daniella knows that I am here.

"I'm exhausted, but yeah, I'm ok!" I am happy to be alive. Daniella looks at me oddly, then looks out to sea.

I turn my head and look down the beach. At any given moment, you can find a few dead jellyfish that have washed ashore and lie motionless. Seaweeds ensnare them, extinguishing their movement like throwing a wet blanket on a smoldering flame. As I look down the beach, I see one not far from where I have landed in the sand.

The jellyfish looks like he had a much harder struggle than I did. "I know, man, I know," I mumble. I sit up, put my wobbly legs underneath me and grab my pack. I put Daniella's hand in mine. We head out for our final dinner together, and I pretend it is just another day at the beach.

Week Thirteen | Finality

Daniella and I both left Tamarindo this morning, but we are leaving on different buses heading in opposite directions. She left for Germany and I went to an arbitrary corner of the country to spend my final four days sulking. Enjoy your life, sweet, silly girl. I hope to one day see you again, but I know I never will.

My soul cracked today. I spent two hours on a bus, in the back row, stretched out on the floor. I don't want to be seen or be heard. I don't want to speak or be spoken to. I need to mend my heart. It is heavy.

I've been everywhere I want to be in this country, twice, but I haven't hiked up an active volcano yet. I need one last hoorah, one last jolt to the soul.

It's late afternoon when I arrive at the volcano affectionately named The Little Old Lady, find a bed and throw my pack down. I grab my guidebook and my smokes and head out the door.

I walk to the nearest stream to sit and listen to Sweet Jane. It's already 4 pm and it's a seven-kilometer hike to the summit. The Lady is a few thousand meters high. I don't think I can make it up and back before sundown. It's supposed to be an overnight trip.

I stand at the trailhead looking up. Here at the base, I know what I must do, I must keep going. I don't have any water with me, but I have a map in the guidebook. That's good enough - it is time to explore!

One couple motions to me to stop. They want to talk. "Don't go, its super windy up there! There is no visibility." Those sentiments perfectly describe my general path throughout life. I'll be fine.

I start walking faster, I am looking for my new wind. I break into a jog, and then a steady run straight up the trail. My mind wanders back to MonteVerde and to Amy. I am back in the Marine Corps climbing Mount Motherfucker. I am battling demons in Spokane. I am at the crystal pools with Daniella. I am not here to enjoy the scenery, rather I am here to mourn and find direction. I occasionally glance at other hikers coming down, but they all look at me like I'm insane so I'll just avoid eye contact.

One man yells out "Tiene agua?" No, I don't have any water. He has gentle eyes and wants wellness for me. He gives me his bottle and wishes me luck. I am without a pack or any gear, running full speed up this volcano as the dusk races down the horizon. I am pushing my limits. I am cleansing my heart. I am being stupid.

After forty-minute of pushing my endurance, I begin to pass bubbling gray mud pits, thermal baths, and steaming holes in the ground. I find boulders and ropes that are here to help me ascend the rock face. The ropes are well used, but still very strong and help me to the top. A short ten-minute hike later, the world changes.

The earth is scorched. I must be walking on old lava. It is course and porous, sharp enough to slice me should I fall. Gusts of wind stop me in my tracks, but I bend my knees and dig in, headstrong into the grayness.

The sulfur is thick, the poisonous clouds obscure my vision and make my eyes burn again. I walk a little further and the clouds begin to dissipate. The wind still thrashes, but I can see the crater now. I can also see the edges of my trail now. One side steeply slopes down the mountain, and the other side is nearly a vertical drop into the depths. I'm here. Time to go home now.

The wind shifts, and my escape rope is now downwind from the crater gasses. There's no time to walk all the way around the crater, but I must get back to the ropes. I must go through. I squint my eyes, tuck my head, and enter the sulfur cloud again. I cover my mouth, put my head down, and try not to get blown into the chasm as I try to ignore the burning sensation in my throat.

I find my favorite stack of rocks. The red ribbon is tied around its girth, fluttering violently in the heavy wind. I find the rope and drop out of the noxious fumes and away from the depths of the chasm.

In the dim dusk glow, I see fog settling on the trails below. As I descend, the mountain air rinses my eyes, but my throat is still like sandpaper. I reach the fog line and breathe in the moist air like an elixir coating my pipes.

I need to get down and find some water. Better yet, I need to catch my flight back to Alaska. I am healed and ready for the next gentle breeze.

I am going home.

Constructing Constants

11

Spring Morphisms

I'm 24 years old I've escaped the grasp of the Marine Corps and the tighter grip of addiction. I now consider myself a proud Alaskan. This new life path feels right, but it is easy to acquiesce when fate is performing her own course corrections.

These long work hours and the sacrifice of my play time are a small price to pay to appease my fate. The path to bliss is unclear - treading through sorrow with no vision of tomorrow - but with the right guide, I may survive another year.

The plane from San Jose lands in Seattle, the northern tip of my triangle. Gavin's brother Jude lives here now and we need to connect, but I also want a place to sleep tonight, it's been a long flight. Jude is like my brother too, without judgement, blind to the vices and my near demise in Spokane. We drink cheap beer from his balcony downtown and stare at the Space Needle.

I buy a bus ticket to Spokane. I know what I need to do. This path is littered with land mines, but I know where they are. I put them there. My mission is to navigate, treading lightly and stepping with care, to my future in the north, where I know I am safe. I will only stay a few weeks - or maybe a month – then buy my ticket to Anchorage and get back to dreaming.

I need to reacquaint myself with America and bind who I was then with who I am now. I need to measure my person, but I also need to keep away from the edges, I can't get swept out with the undertow. It is time to see my constants and sniff at my limits, but I won't become tangled again in Spokane.

The Triangle is a critical part of decompressing. It grounds me back to the constants of my homeland with whom I've been separated for so long. The triangle is also an adventure, only dipped in the comforts of home.

The familiar scenery prances by the window, reminding me that I am near my friends, my family, and other relationships I have tested. These times are also when reflection is brightest. Sitting on these long buses, the introspection digs deepest, and the buried memories bubble to the surface.

This time in Spokane, I am safe. I am Smart. Gavin buys beers and takes me to punk shows. The cockroaches that used to live here have all scurried back into the walls. The sun is shining, and the river is flowing. A week passes, and I come to rest in The Town So Nice, Walla Walla. Like Spokane, the plan is to make a quick visit, then bus back to Seattle and catch a plane to Alaska, but my father has other plans.

My father and I have always taken road trips, ever since I was just a peewee. We drove all over Washington going to horse shows and hockey games. We drove down to California together for skate camp, we even went to Yellowstone. It comes as no surprise that he wants to drive me to Alaska, four days and 2,500 miles away.

Before I flew to Costa Rica four months ago, I stashed $200 at my parents' house to guarantee my one-way ticket back to Anchorage. Since I'm now driving with dad, I can use this money otherwise. I am improving upon my first destitute trip to Kenai, but there is still much work to be done with my planning skills.

The Alcan, the Alaska-Canada Highway, passes through British Columbia and the Yukon provinces of Canada, before crossing into Alaska, the largest state in our united union. It's late March. At best, the roads are still wet. At worst, they are layered with ice.

At the end of the first day, we are deep into British Columbia. It's late in the evening when we roll into the town of Prince George for a snore. I recline the passenger seat, throw a blanket over my legs and fall fast asleep. Dad does likewise. Every hour we start the car so we can turn on the heater. It then takes about an hour to cool down. Repeat as necessary.

After about six hours of restless wiggling, the sun pokes its nose into our little pickup truck. I open one eye, acknowledge its presence, and then go back to sleep. My father is slightly more restless or perhaps he just likes to drive. He turns the key and my bed comes to a slow rumble. We back out of the rest stop and roar further down the road. A few hours pass. After breakfast, we are ready for day two. eight more hours pass before we pull into the halfway point of our trip.

The road to Valdez is conveniently spaced between vast expanses. If we drive 700 miles a day, the Liard River Hot Springs are perfectly poised at the end of the second day. As we arrive, we see the chilly air steaming off the warm rock-lined springs. The area is well manicured, sitting amidst tall pines and granite boulders. We replace our road clothes with swim gear, and step into the warm sulfur springs. Fatigue and dirt are sucked from our bodies and put back into the Earth, waiting to be reclaimed somewhere down the road on a different day.

My father and I sleep well after soaking in Earth's treatment, even if we're still huddled in this truck. We will drive this road together four more times over the coming years, and we will always make it our mission to divide the tour in half at Liard Hot Springs.

Through the third day and most of the fourth, the scenery is beautiful but stagnant. The trees line the highways for hundreds of miles between the small towns, interrupted only by lakes and the occasional chain saw artist selling tree trucks carved into natures scenes. There is burly mountain-man history in these parts. The Klondike Gold Rush came through here a hundred years ago, and they still regularly celebrate this prosperous past.

The old growth forests of Seattle have mostly been replaced by prickly evergreens that carpet the timberland. Every few hours, we find a new lake where we can pull off and take a break alongside other road-weary campers.

The highways cut through vast stretches of land. Coming down the hills, we can see for miles to the bottom of the mountain, across the flat bottom, and back up the other side. This balances the need for speed with the need to not meet the police. Like life, there is no place to hide.

After four days of driving to Valdez, it would be a luxury to finally arrive at my house, complete with a real bed and shower. Unfortunately, such a place does not exist for me. I still live out of my decrepit van left vacant in a field. It is a shelter with walls, nothing more, but it suffices. I live in my body, not my van or my barn.

On the road into town, about an hour from our destination, we pass Thompson's Pass, where my friends jump off of cliffs on snowboards and snow machines. I show my dad Tsaina Lodge, the only place within miles if we need warmth, food, or alcohol.

We pass old-town Valdez, the site of the city before it fell into the ocean during the earthquake of 1964. We come upon the only street light in town. It is green, signaling we are good to go.

At the end of last summer, I never moved my van to a secure location, I know of no secure locations. I just left it where it was, hoping that it wouldn't get towed or stolen. I'm not sure if it is still there. I don't really care, it's more of a convenience, it has served its purpose. If I need to, I can park my new tent on Hippy Hill by the canneries.

My van welcomes me home from the precise corner of the field where I left it at the end of last summer. I can't possibly play host to my Dad under these circumstances, but we have been sleeping in the truck for four days. Our definition of normal is inconsistent.

Dad pulls his truck up alongside my van and we now have a duplex. The cold has frozen the scene and preserved all motor functions. My van sputters but still starts. I get out of dad's truck and prepare to sleep in my own home, while dad does likewise in his truck.

I was unclear if my father would find this lifestyle as liberating as I do, but he does have an equal appreciation for adventure. He thinks it's cute. We spend a few days seeing the best parts of Valdez and play a few games of pool with my winter friends. We visit the harbor mixed with houseboats and sea trawlers getting ready to set out. We have some drinks at the Sugarloaf, where I introduce him to my friends Al, Reba, Bud, Beau, and a few others of my new constants.

When we wake, we share our final breakfast, exchange manly hugs, and shake hands. Dad gets into his little pickup and leaves Valdez, headed for Kenai. I cannot go with him. It saddens me that he won't be coming back to the land's edge in Valdez before he drives for four more days back through Canada, by himself, to get home. I will see him in Walla Walla after the summer passes- six months and a lifetime away.

Just like the last two seasons, I am here too early. Most of the snow is still in big piles in the parking lots. After dad leaves, I still have six weeks to get settled in before the masses arrive in Valdez for the tourist season.

The excitement of living alone in a snowy field, in an old van, quickly fades. I move. My new parking lot is at the harbor, halfway through the U-shaped spit, between the boats and the narrow beach on the opposing side. I am home. I am isolated, but still close to everything.

A few deserted boats bobble in the water in front of me. Big Al's restaurant is a two-minute walk past the harbor master and the showers. In the other direction, I see Cannery Row, where I first landed with Colin and the group of nine. I need to see some new activity. It's lonely out here waiting for workers and tourists to brighten the days and help make life social. It still feels like winter.

Since I arrived four weeks ago, I have been the only vehicle in this entire harbor parking lot. Now a few new trucks have pulled in during the evening darkness to work on their boats. They leave me in peace, although I wouldn't reject a conversation if it came to that.

I've been helping Al get his restaurant ready for the summer crowds in exchange for meals and a sense of loyalty to one another. Share a winter with anyone in Alaska and they become instant family.

The winters are rough, the springtime is pleasant, and the summers are pure bliss. My monthly bills are about $20. The small propane tank for my lantern is $4, while the larger tank for my heater costs $6. Both tanks need to be replaced every few weeks. I need to hire a butler to handle these things.

The ice is cracking, and the days are stretching. Fresh faces and new hip fishies come into town. I know them. Only one winter, a summer, and one more winter separate me from their experience. As I started in Kenai with Cole, so begins their journey here on Cannery Row.

I never gave it much thought before, but I need to do some housekeeping and general interior decorating. My van needs some curtains, or rather, I need some privacy. There is now light traffic at the harbor and it will only get busier. The stinky mattress sits directly on the cold metal. There is no layer of carpeting, and the walls are bare skeletons exposing their ribs.

The wheel wells are corroded, and I can see through to the snow below. When people are wandering outside and I have to pee, these holes also double as my latrine. I'm not a Cretan though, I piss in a plastic bottle first, then pour it through the hole. The human spirit learns to adapt and overcome.

I am comfortable knowing that I will no longer be slinging fish, I have graduated to cooking them. These new faces, with their tents and packs, they still feel like my kin even if they stink more than I ever did. The air surrounding them is a bitter mix of slime, salt water and sweat all blended in with the smell of plastic raingear. It is a familiar smell, but I am above that now. I smell of tobacco, dirt, and propane.

Valdez is a small, somber little town, but it does have a second-hand store. I buy shower rods and use some old sheets as curtains. I also buy the thickest blanket I can find and throw it on the floor. I don't want my van to give me tetanus while I sleep.

My summer is set. I will sleep in this wheeled bucket, eat at Al's, and shower at the quarter-operated harbor-master facilities. There's also a laundromat across from the Sugarloaf. I'm thirty seconds from the beach where we will have our bonfires, and all the bars are within a ten-minute walk. Home.

I am happy to see Bud and tell him of my time outside the country, to tell him of the people I met, and the lands I crossed. Reba is still here too, along with most of my winter friends who thrived in the snow.

Chuck is the brawniest mountain climber I've ever known. He climbs Mount McKinley every year, and has ascended three of the twelve highest peaks, even making one unsuccessful attempt at Everest. It takes a strong mind to do these things, especially after losing three toes to frostbite.

Chuck is hardcore, reclusive, and now dead. On a dark night last February, he was walking home from the Sugarloaf when he sat down, passed out, and froze to death. This is the polar opposite of how I spent my winter, frolicking in sand and worrying about the undertow.

Death by bar hopping happens to someone every year. For me, a different path will fulfill the seasonal cycle. My winter must be filled with revolutions and revelations, with magic and misery, with life and vibrancy. I cannot stay here and become a popsicle like Chuck.

As the summer gains steam, I return to the familiar restaurant scene, harassing the waitresses and burning my fingers. I have completed my first full revolution and am returned fresh with a purpose.

There are only five strong months of summer work. I need to save as many thousands of dollars as possible. I must cook breakfast, lunch, and dinner and forego the luxuries of Kenai, Soldotna, and Hippy Hill. I must flip the switch and get busy!

For months, new faces come and other faces go, as the summer breathes with life. Bonds strengthen throughout the season, but the party is ending. The lights are coming on and the summer is closing. We are in that short period of the northern light cycle, when dawn stretches from twilight into a standard ten-hour nighttime. It is time to go, it's only getting darker.

The plan is to fly into Quito, Ecuador, and traverse down the spine of the continent, the Andes Mountains. Just to the west, I can go to the beaches. And the Amazon

Rainforest is to the East. The ancient city of Machu Pichu will be my shining beacon at the end of this long road.

I hold no reservations. I will be in South America for $4,500 and not a dollar more. Time measures money, and mine is set at $25 per day. This will allow me six months away.

When the money runs out, so does my time. I'm optimistic, and I need to stop getting to Alaska so damn early. It is neither my destiny to come home to an Alaskan winter, nor to get stuck in South America working for local wages. The wind must not push me too far from the path, but I am allowed a moderate turbulence.

I land in Quito just after Halloween and will leave from Peru next March. Flying into one end and out the other, I will not be tethered to a singular point on the map like I was in Costa Rica.

Cultures are the lifeblood of the nations, but the commerce resonates, and the traffic emanates from the capital cities. This is where I plant my temporary roots with the pretense of permanence, but without the accompanying strings of consequence.

The paths that await, bind us to our fate, but some paths walk themselves. God's gift of clarity will now show me my first steps.

My Mind on Quinine

12

Week One

Taxi drivers descend in procession after I clear customs at Mariscal Sucre International Airport in Quito, Ecuador. I find one I trust and throw my pack in the backseat. He sets his meter and we careen towards old town. This is the moment. This is why I travel. There is a new world just outside my door. I've made it!

My arrival to South America coincides with the week-long Founding of Quito celebration. The city is awash with fireworks and street stalls, human statues and sidewalk painters. I imagine my arrival to South America has prompted this festive music and celebration. The vibes give me the impression that the entire city is happy to see me. After all, it is also my Independence Day.

The Gran Casino is a backpacker dive in a shanty part of Quito. This offers me the security of being surrounded amongst fellow travelers. It is also in an area where dark things lurk in the alleys. It takes ten minutes to check in and drop off my pack.

It would probably be wise to rest a little since I just got here, but I don't have that wisdom. It's time to debark from the flying ship, meet the natives, and drink their ale. I trot back outside to my awaiting taxi, ready to take me downtown.

We spiral through downtown, arriving at the juicy center. The night air blends with the crumbling suburbs until eventually the neon signs come into view. I know where the night life is, it beckons me like gravity.

I quickly find the groove, the night is right, the mood is electric. El Pub has an old western feel, with a long wooden bar encompassed by round stools. Drunken patrons circle the dance floor, while dancers tear a hole in the center of the room.

The Merengue and Salsa beats echo across the walls in crisp unison with the strobe lights. The wooden rafters match those of small barns, reminiscent of my childhood. Leaning against the bar, I scan the crowd and slam my beer. "Una mas, por favor!" The bartender brings me a beer.

Across the room, my eye meets another. I study her, and the people around her. Everyone is smiling and this makes me smile too. She sees me staring. Our energies collide and she walks my way.

"Quieres bailar?" Oh crap, I don't dance, not like this! The couples are spinning so fast the floorboards are turning into sawdust. "I speak some English," she says. "My name is Jimena."

She is Morena, with slightly darker skin and traits from the highlands, but her family is now local to Quito. She has kind eyes and high cheekbones, forcing her face into an enduring smile.

We drink shots of tequila together and dance slowly for hours. As our evening ends, we collect contact info and vow to meet again. I jump in a taxi.

"Hasta tomorrow," I wave out the window to Jimena as I drive away. I am anxious to collapse in my room and wrestle away the jet lag and tequila.

Morning breaks on my first day in South America, but I have time, I go back to sleep until I awake in the afternoon. I throw on some clothes, zip up my pack, and head out to cash some traveler's cheques.

I may look for another apartment today, that worked well in Costa Rica. There also might be an artisan market somewhere, that could be fun tonight. Maybe I'll just get lost in a festival. I walk across most of Quito and see what I can find.

The first thing I did last year was to take some Spanish classes. This worked to integrate me into both the local culture and the western traveler's culture. The classes are not only to enhance my Spanish, but also to help me plant roots, learn, and make a plan. I intend to blend since will be here for a while.

In the months of anxiety back in Alaska, while waiting to come here, I did my research. I know where I want to go. Now that I'm on the right continent, I just have to walk for three hours across town, past a residential area, and across another park.

The short path up the sidewalk leads me to a buzzer mounted to a black spiky fence which could easily impale a trespasser if they tried to climb it. Other sections of the wall are topped with shards of broken soda bottles embedded in the concrete.

The gate leads to a short walkway permeated with rich green grass. If I were a horse, this lawn would be the perfect snack. The house at the end of the walkway is small but welcoming. A slender man about a decade older than me walks out and meets me at the gate.

"Te ayudo, can I help you?" The man says in both languages, indicating that I am indeed in the right place.

"Busco un escuela!" The professor knows why I am here, I need a Spanish school. After exchanging pleasantries in English, we step inside the house.

"For $10 per day we provide three hours of Spanish instruction by local people your age. For another $10 per day, we have a room upstairs you can stay in. We have other Europeans staying here too." I instantly commit. This will still leave $6 per day for food and entertainment. I leave my ghetto hostel and move into the gated house on the opposite side of town.

Week Two | *The Ascent*

I met Carl at the Founding-Day parties, but those parties have now dwindled, and the firework dust has settled. Even though I've moved to the suburbs to go to school, we still hang out. Carl is slightly taller than I am and somewhere around thirty. He isn't nearly as handsome as I am though.

Carl's brash nature matches his appearance. He wears a wiry beard that fails to hide his acne-scarred skin. Birds would find a happy home in his natty hair. He smells sour, like he lives on a diet of vinegar and garlic. He's underfed but energetic. He is skinny just like me. It must be something in the food we aren't eating.

Carl is adventurous, experienced, and confident of his plans, again like me. However, unlike me, he knows why he is here. He has a reason to be in Ecuador. I'm just here to see where the wind blows. I'll grab onto his coat tails to see where they will whip me.

Mount Cotopaxi sits two hours south of Quito. It is Earth's highest active volcano, at 20,000 feet vertical from sea level. The Incas believe that God lives at the top, but I don't think they are talking about Jesus' Dad. The Andes are already at a breathtaking elevation, but Cotopaxi sits like a breast with a large white nipple on the naked body of the high plains. We are going to climb her.

Carl is smart, he's a climber back in Colorado, he knows we must first practice before we climb Cotopaxi. Quito is second highest capital in the world and Carl's been here for a month to acclimatize. He's been preparing

125

his body and mind to climb Cotopaxi and a few other peaks down the Andes range. I've been in this country for a week and have been drunk the whole time. I'm unsure of what this altitude will do to me, but I have fortitude. As a heavy smoker, I'm not sure what I'm thinking, but I'm going to climb Cotopaxi with Carl.

On Saturday, we catch a bus to Aloasi, home to El Corazon, one of the other peaks along the Avenida de Volcanos de la Cordillera Occidental. This is just a warm-up climb Cotopaxi, but El Corazon is still 15,000 feet high, a feat in its own rite.

The trip can be completed in just one day starting from Quito. The guidebooks say it is "easy but potentially deadly." I have an ex-girlfriend that fits that description. Carl and I just need to stay away from the deadly parts and close to the easy parts and we will survive. It's not like anyone has ever died from climbing volcanoes, not really.

Our practice trek up El Corazon is just an exhausting hike with some rock scrambling near the crater. The view from the summit overlooks vast farm lands and sweeping views of the two Illiniza peaks, Sur y Norte. Behind us, looming overhead, we see our next climb. We now feel ready for the real thing. We will climb Mount Cotopaxi in seven days.

When we get back to Quito, we schedule our trip with Carl's guide and listen to stories of those that went before us. Despite the cutesy Quechua name meaning *Neck of the Moon*, Cotopaxi is real mountaineering and legitimately quite dangerous.

"Five weeks ago, an avalanche broke loose from the crater rim, rolled all the way back to base camp and killed thirteen people," our guide informs us. I don't believe him, I would have heard about that, but Carl looks serious. Our guide also tells us that only one in three treks will summit all the way to the crater. The final hour has dangerous crevasses and overhangs that can release walls of snow if they are disturbed. "Wait, what!"

It's time. Carl and I arrive at the tourist shop at noon to our awaiting guides. We throw our day packs into his truck, climb in, and head south out of the city. It's a quick three-hour drive to base camp, but we need to be asleep early tonight. We will ascend Cotopaxi tomorrow before the sun does.

We stop once to collect another couple on the way, not that Carl and I are a couple, just to be clear. We stop again for two more climbers, and then drive through the arid Incan highlands towards the volcano.

Our team consists of six climbers with three guides. One guide will watch base camp while the other two will take us to the top. The afternoon is spent learning how to use our crampons and our ice axes. There's an ice sheet directly behind our base-camp cabin. We climb up fifty feet and slide down on our bellies, simulating an actual fall. We practice digging our axes into the hard ice to slow our descents.

The crampons are like scant bear traps stuck to my feet, but without their grip I wouldn't get very far. If I start sliding on my belly, it's important to use the axe, not the crampons! If I start sliding and dig my crampons into the ice, I would end up doing cartwheels. That is an entirely different skill set that I do not possess.

At 5 pm, the guides tell us to get some sleep. This is about eight hours before my usual bedtime, but our bodies now need rest and acclimation. This isn't about mental recovery, like a simple hangover, this is about endurance and survival.

Morning comes quickly. Carl and I exit the shack into the darkness. The snowline seems intentionally placed directly behind base-camp, dimly lit by the sliver of a moon. We bundle with layers of jackets and meet with the rest of the party behind the hut. The air is invigorating, but calm and inviting.

We don our helmets and strap the bear traps to our feet. We try not to blind each other with our headlamps while we search around in the dark and brisk morning. Stepping into our harnesses permits the guides to thread a rope through our carabineers, shackling us together into a millipede procession ready to succeed or fail as a unit. If one falls - we all fall.

Our ascent starts at 2 am. I give my goggles a final adjustment and put on my gloves. Lit by a faint equatorial night sky, the trail is easy to find: it is straight up. We begin the slippery walk with the appropriate lack of fervor at this early morning hour.

Our headlamps project small circles onto the sheen of ice, scurrying in the white like little glowing mice. As the hours pass, we begin to shine our lights squarely at the ground in front of us. We walk single file in each other's footsteps, pressing each other's imprints deeper into the snow. The hours pass, the incline increases, and the air thins. I grasp the rope that binds us together, but the strength in my grip is fading. It is reminiscent of Captain Jim's set net in Kenai, aching from the core.

As the pace slows to match our muscle strength and oxygen intake, the team feels the strain. We grow fatigued, while the remaining climbers adjust their speeds to compensate. It will need to be a collective achievement to reach the top of this behemoth.

Our guides herd us up the ridge for hours, until we eventually come to a stop and rest in a semi-circle on a small ice shelf. Our guides remind us that if the numbness and shortness of breath become unbearable, one guide can take us down as the other explorers may still press upward with the other guide. If someone else wants to descend later, the trip is over for everyone. The team cannot continue with no guides, that would be as foolish as me being here in the first place.

Although we are offered an opportunity for the pain to end now, we decide to continue upward as a cohesive team. We are closer to the top than we are to the bottom. Ten minutes pass. We stop again in a futile effort to catch our breath.

Hiking Cotopaxi is like moonwalking in a hall of mirrors, while the oxygen is being slowly sucked from the hallway. The intermissions for inspiration grow more frequent as the day elapses and the footprints fade behind us. The summit seems increasingly unattainable. We've been climbing for hours and it seems no closer.

Breathe, step, rest. Breathe, step, rest. Our ice axes pierce the hard snow in partnership with our crampons, pulling us forward against gravity's grip. Grumbles of encouragement bond our tribe and deter any thoughts of descending just to end the pain. I'll keep my thoughts of turning around to myself, although I'm sure that the team's encouragement is meant for me.

After ten hours of grueling monotony in near darkness, we begin the steepest and most difficult pass. The route is simplistic, not overly technical, just exhausting. There is also a real danger of sliding down this mountainside. The path is full of slippery switchbacks, with no trees to obscure our way, provide landmarks, or to break our fall. Everything is just gray, inside and out.

The fog is thick, but we trudge on. The two guides flank our sides. We are six hikers connected at the hip, bundled in winter gear, turning our heads down to avoid the wind. Our headlamps shine on the feet in front of us.

The summit grows closer and the distance between the neighboring peaks extend as the mountains funnel upwards. Once we pass the cloud-line, the sun begins to shine. The view opens around us like the unveiling of the curtains at The Ritz.

Our struggle is over, it's no longer necessary to motivate each other, instead, the volcano motivates each of us independently, as we sit in awe upon a flat terrace a few hundred meters from the crater.

The sun rises to greet us and to warm our faces. We sit in a row upon the snow, sharing hugs, smiles, and a sense of accomplishment. I look at the team and every face is exhilarated. Eyes of wonder, tire, and satisfaction hang below ice-frosted eyebrows.

The guides gather us in a semi-circle. "Como estan, todos? Everybody good?" We all nod in agreement as we sit upon the glacier, eat our fiber bars, and bask in the sun which is just now cresting over El Corazon. "This es el fin, the end. Llegamos! Congratulations!"

I look around, I see no crater.

"The summit path is there," he says pointing towards a snowy ledge. "But it looks no bueno. We can go a little closer, but this es el fin." We're here.

The path to the top leads to an unstable overhang that looks like it could rip apart from the mountain at any moment. We are unable to continue to the summit, lest we risk an unplanned descent surfing on the back of an avalanche. The crater's ridges are evident, but we can't see inside. We don't care though. We are sitting perched on God's window, looking out across the Andes.

We are all still breathless, but it is not from the lack of oxygen at this altitude but rather in awe of the vast expanse that spreads out beneath us. The satisfaction we all now share can only be formed through our collective effort. We are all part of a much larger machine, a cohesive chain, physically linked to one another.

We descend the mountain in synchronicity with the sun, arriving back at base camp just as day blends into dusk. The mood of our group is one of elation, but the day has been long. After an hour of decompression and packing, we pile into our pickup truck and sleep the entire route back to Quito.

Six more weeks pass leisurely, visiting the countryside and the discotecas. Jimi and I take weekend excursions to the mountains or down to the coast. The acclimatizing phases are over, I am integrated. My feet are starting to itch, and my spare hours are spent reading my guidebook, looking for what comes next. The options in Ecuador are thinning like the Cotopaxi air, I'm looking towards Peru.

We are in Otavalo, a small village a few hours north of Quito. This is the largest market in Ecuador, where we will spend our precious Sucres. I buy a few trinkets, and then sit under the umbrellas drinking juice and chatting with Jimena. We don't have an agenda, that's what's nice about markets. That's what's nice about traveling and life in general. Freedom from concern, no strings, no dependencies and no addictions. My mind begins to wander to my past sins, to all the steps that have brought me to this Valhalla.

As if she were telepathic, right on cue, Jimi asks "Quieres coca? Do you want some?"

"Como? Que?" I wonder how she knows I like cocaine. We haven't talked about Spokane yet, my past life is still behind me, isolated from this fairytale.

She points to a vendor with bags of small stiff leaves. Here in the Andes, the coca leaf is used for its natural medicinal properties, before it is tainted, turned into cocaine and sold to the west. The plant is picked in Ecuador, transported to Peru for processing into a paste, then shipped north again to Columbia to become powder.

In Ecuador, coca is still just a leaf. It is a blood thinner to combat altitude sickness from the lack of atmospheric pressure in the high Andes. It helps your blood flow and your body to function. My blood is fine, the elevation doesn't bother me, I just want to get high.

Our bag of leaves comes with a little gray stone the size of a marble. It is brittle, and flakes away when scraped with a knife. Jimena lays four leaves flat upon a tree stump, overlapping at their centers, fanning them into the shape of a star. Jimi grabs my knife and scrapes shavings from the stone into the center of the star.

Jimi folds the leaves around the shavings and wraps it into a tight package. She puts it in my mouth and instructs me to chew it lightly. The shavings from the enzyme stone activate the properties of plant, making my mouth tingle. This is neat. I think I'll hold onto this enzyme stone and bag of leaves for a little while.

Our day at the Otovalo market comes to its end, but before we go, Jimi wants to get a shirt for her younger brother. She wanders into the market, leaving me sitting on a tree stump, chewing my coca pouch, with a bag of leaves in my hand, when one of the most engrossing people approaches me.

She looks like she's lived eighty hard Andean years. She is draped in a burlap cloak, hunched over like death. Her loose-fitting hood is draped across her face. As she walks toward me, her hood billows in a breeze, exposing the other half of her face. Her skin is decayed and peeled away but scarred into permanence. She was a victim of leprosy or some other flesh-eating virus.

She approaches. Her mouth is closed, yet I can clearly see her teeth. One solid white eye is perched atop her exposed cheekbone like a moon that will never set. She extends her hand, palms upturned, and says "Sucres?"

I now realize why the name of the Ecuadorian currency sounds familiar. Sucres (money) reminds me of words like azucar (sugar) and sangre (blood). Thankfully, this lady just wants my money, not my sugar or my blood. But still, I am startled. As a mere reflex, I extend my hand and offer her my bag of leaves and my neat little stone.

She knows she caught me by surprise. She lifts her hand and gently pushes the bag back towards me. She fixes her hood and disappears back into the market. It is evident that not everyone at this market is on an extended holiday from Alaska to buy useless trinkets.

I sit on my stump and reflect on my privilege. Why do my steps merit me luxuries while she wanders half blind and without a coin? I ponder karma, and wish I paid the reaper with cash instead of offering her drugs.

Week Six

Jimena wants to go to Baños this weekend to see a famous concert at the Founding of Baños festival. This raises a few questions. Does every place in Ecuador have a *Founding of this Town* day and why name a city *Baños*? Baños means 'bathroom' in Spanish, so I ask the question. Apparently, it translates closer to baths than to bathroom, since the foothills are dotted by thermal pools that are warmed by nearby volcanoes.

I concede to Jimena and here we now sit, in Baños. This is a nice weekend escape away from the city, but I've been to many of these festivals over the last month. On the second day, I find the sign - the omen - that will light my next pathway.

Although I feel local, there is yet another step to be taken to enter the indigenous world. I am not yet immersed enough. Strolling the streets of Baños, I spot a piece of paper tucked away at the bottom of a full-size window of a nondescript restaurant. It reads:

EXPEDICIÓN A PARQUE YASUNI
– SECTOR HOURANI –

On the right side of the paper, there is a picture of a short-haired Amazon tribesman holding a blowgun. The other side of the paper outlines the five-day itinerary into the jungle to explore and experience the life of this tribe.

I know of the Hourani. I was once inspired by a documentary that outlined how they are a peaceful hunting tribe that had been infiltrated for the oil flowing beneath their soil.

The Hourani oppose all external influences equally. They demand and deserve their isolation. Their warriors attempted to chase helicopters away with spears, tragically ending with most of the Hourani shot dead.

The Coordinator of the First Hourani National Assembly wrote the following open letter to the Ecuadorian government:

"We don't want to see tour guides or tourists because they bring diseases that the Hourani can't cure. They enter our houses when we are hunting or working in the fields. They hunt and fish for the food we need, and they leave us garbage. Tourists are paying but we are being exploited and receive nothing. Therefore, we resist tourism. If necessary, we will oppose tourism with our spears."

– Hourani Elder

When I left Quito for another Founding party two days ago, I packed only enough for the two days in Baños and brought only enough cash to get back to Quito. All my camping equipment is stored under my bed, and my travelers' checks are in the school safe. Regardless, I am always curious.

I enter the café and Jimi follows. I find the owner, and ask "Whose tour? How much? When does it leave?"

"I have his number, I will call him." She does. "He can be here in one hour, he'll answer your questions." She leaves me with an ardent sense of curiosity without a single answer. We must return in an hour.

After a brief stroll around the village, we return to investigate. As we enter, a fit local in his thirties stands and approaches us. He is friendly but wears the uniform of a successful street hustler: jeans, polo shirt, white Nike shoes, well-groomed with a mustache, and a silly grin.

"Hola, I Primo." He introduces himself, and we do likewise. "You interest in la jungla or adventura?" His English is decent, but we quickly convert to Spanish.

"Absolutely. It's to see the Hourani? I thought they didn't accept visitors?" I question him on the safety of this venture, and he assures me that the tribes are paid fairly. They won't throw spears at us if we remain respectful.

"When do you leave?"

"Tomorrow night, we need more people." He says staring intently, trying to drag a positive response from my gaze. I look at Jimi and she looks disappointed. She knows what comes next, and she can't be part of it. I now find myself the casualty of an exceptional opportunity, surrendering to my impulse reflexes.

Plans always change, but I am learning how to embrace these changes. Jimi is now going back to Quito by herself. I am going to play in the jungle. I'm kind of a bad boyfriend, but she understands my purpose.

Primo only needs one more person for the tour and I sense his desperation. He can't make the trip without a fourth traveler, it wouldn't be worth it for him if there were only three.

"I left all my cash in Quito!" I tell him. "I only brought enough for the weekend and a little extra."

"How much extra?" He questions.

"I can pay $60." This is less than half of his asking price of $150 for the week-long trek.

"Pero food, fuel, time, and pay chief! $60 not enough." He breaks from Spanish protocol and pleads with me in broken English. His look of disappointment mirrors that of Jimi. I've managed to disappoint Jimi through desertion, and now I've disappointed Primo by being destitute. The mood was happier an hour ago.

I start to walk away. "Ok. You pay me half now, send me half later," Primo says, willing to deal.

"I don't have half, I only have $60." This is not negotiable, that only gives me $20 left in my pocket. He eventually understands and we seal the deal. We'll meet tomorrow at 8pm in front of this café.

In the morning, I put Jimi on the bus to Quito, and waste my day waiting for nighttime to descend. I don't have money, my girlfriend, or my camping gear, but two of those three things aren't needed where I am going.

Evening falls. At the café, I join two girls from Chile and an Ecuadorian guy named Diego. He lives in Miami but has come back to explore his homeland. Oh, I'm here too, I make four.

Having six months to play on this continent, I always planned to visit the jungles of South America. Before leaving home, I was sure to take my yellow fever shots and my doses of Quinine pills – or maybe it was Larium. My long-term preparations for this trip were atypically astute, I just didn't realize it was all happening this weekend. Time and plans are noble, until they walk up to you and say *"Now!"*

These Quinine pills have profound side effects. The prescribed dosage is to take one per week, starting four weeks before any jungle trip, then continue until I've been out for four weeks. The World Health Organization would later retract and announce that Quinine should not be taken for long periods of time to prevent malaria. That approach only masks the symptoms, which is even more dangerous. Instead, the suggested regimen is to wait until you get malaria - and then dose heavy on the way to a hospital. I'm on the hybrid plan, I'll take more if I get sick.

The side-effects of this long-term exposure are surreal and perpetuated on a weekly basis. Quinine permeates the spinal fluid and interacts with the central nervous system. It makes my skin tingle and my hair feels like rubber bands. My dreams are lucid, and they blend into the day's reality. My waking mind is dancing with my subconscious, blurring the lines between the wanted and the realized.

The route through the national park to the village is complicated and requires several different modes of transport. We must first get to Coca, 300 km north on a muddy, rutted road. The main highway runs North-South through the country, but we are nowhere near that luxury. Instead, we traverse the Troncal Amazonica - the trunk of the Amazon. This arterial road feeds the rural areas.

Just three miles outside of Baños, we get our first flat tire. About an hour later – another. Each time, we are back on the road almost as swiftly as we had come to rest. These drivers are prepared for two flat tires, and we just put on the last one. We are barely out of the city and we don't have a spare tire.

The landscape is dark, lush, and wet. El Niño strikes again. The trees and growth stretch into our path, brushing the bus as we drive down the frontage road.

Week Seven | Day Zero

These 300km on backroads were supposed to only take five hours. Instead, it has been *sixteen* hours! We didn't get any more flat-tires last night, but the ruts in the road were grabbing at us, trying to pull us into the earth. We drove very slowly. After endless bumps, jolts, and pot holes, we finally arrive at the bridge to Coca and come to a full stop.

When I awake, I see a small, lazy river in front of our bus. We need to cross about a hundred feet of water, but it looks like the bridge is under construction. There is no more road in front of us! We have reached the end.

I look at the map in my guidebook. There are no other roads into Coca from this side of the bridge. If we don't cross here, we need to go all the way back to Baños.

I look around at my bus companions. The fear and uncertainty also manifest in their faces. "What are we doing?!" I say in Spanish to the local man sitting next to me with a basket in his lap.

"Just wait," he says. I notice his death grip on the armrest as we speak, his fingers curled, and his knuckles wrinkled.

"What are waiting for? The motor is off." He turns to respond, but then suddenly the bus lurches forward!

Did something just nudge us? I look outside in panic. The road just separated from the bank! It seems we parked on a platform, which is now floating on the river!

Staring out the window, I see four monstrous cables pulled tightly across the river spanning from bank to bank. My eyes follow the cables to a huge tree. A massive chain is tied around its girth, securing a pulley about the size of a spare tire to the side of the tree. The cables thread through pulleys, make an about-face, and then end at the platform upon which we now float.

On each side of the bus, a team of men pull on a massive steel cable that loops through the pulley and moves our bus across the river. Opposing forces, equal and opposite, coordinate our passage to the other side.

We're bus surfing! They pull our bus across the river on this plank of a raft, working in perfect unison. This must be synchronized to keep the bus from shifting sideways, becoming like the trucks on the icy Alaskan roads sliding out of control.

I wish I paid more attention to how securely our bus drove onto this platform when we stopped. I cannot see what we are on, only the river flowing around us and a few thick cables. I do not want to drift down the river in a bus on a plank. That is not how I want to see the Ecuadorian Amazon.

El Niño has made the rains fierce, and the rains have turned the ground into thick mud. After successfully surfing the bus to the opposing bank, we dock, and the men tie our platform to two large wooden poles.

The hard part is over, or perhaps not.

Although our raft is now secure, we must now battle the muddy hill to get to flat land. The dirt road is steep and this bus is big.

The driver revs the engine and guns it up the road. We get halfway to the top before our wheels lose traction. The driver slowly returns us back to the platform. After about ten or twelve tries, we finally make it! The bus erupts with cheers and we are now free from the oddities of this river crossing.

Drifting from Customs

13

Week Seven | Day One

We are near to the Columbian border, which explains the numerous passport checks we have been through since we crossed the river. Soldiers are guarding the path against drug traffickers going between these two countries. I have some coca leaves with me, but I don't think that counts. Armed men board our bus to inspect the occupants – that's us.

The soldier doesn't ask for my passport, or even acknowledge my presence. Either my frightened face or my blonde hair divulges that I am not an Ecuadorian escaping to Columbia with drugs.

After passing the fourth checkpoint, I see something I have waited to see since we left Baños sixteen hours ago: pavement!

We arrive in steamy, sweaty Coca. It's a sauna-city, where the barometer reads one notch below liquid air. Immediately after we stop, the locals disperse from the bus like they have an agenda. I team up with Diego, the two Chilean girls, and our guide Primo from Baños. At the Coca bus station, we are met by our second guide, Moipa. He is from this jungle. He is Hourani.

We buy gas and pick up the motor that we will attach to our dugout canoe. It is great that we now have a motor with us, but I am more concerned about where they put the rest of the boat! We can't get there by motor alone.

Diego and I help the guides gather supplies for the ill-planned trip and pack it all into an old Jeep parked outside of the store. The driver is expecting us.

The shop lady comes running out of the store. "WHO'S GONNA PAY FOR THE CHICKEN??" She is irate. Moipa scowls at Primo, and Primo indignantly pays the lady. We leave Coca.

Primo and Moipa sit in the front of the Jeep, while the girls, Diego, and I all sit in the back guarding the supplies. Primo expertly navigates the muddy creviced roads, but I credit the Jeep more than Primo.

After three hours of bouncy back roads, an abysmal vision comes into view. A mile in the distance, a lonely chimney spire juts into the sky above the canopy. An orange flame spews into the air, releasing a trail of thick black smoke that mingles with the clouds.

The presence of this modern-industrial oil refinery reminds me who won the battle between spears and helicopters. I have an epiphany of my hypocrisy and realize that the same petrol that kills the land and its people also powers the Jeep that now takes us deep into their jungle to mingle with their people.

We drive through lush, green vibrancy. The landscape begs to be explored, it is our earth too. We intend to pay the chief to compensate for our visit, but they never needed money until we disrupted their routines. I fear that the discount Primo gave me will come directly out of the chief's bribe.

"Oye, Primo!" I yell to get his attention in the front seat. I call out loud enough to get Moipa's attention too. They both listen attentively. "Do the chief and his tribe still get all of their bounty money, or did we spend their payment on our own groceries?"

Moipa looks at me surprisingly, unaware that we might be short on cash. Moipa looks back intently at Primo. My head is stuck between the two front seats, eagerly awaiting his confirmation.

"Yeah, one price," Primo says in Spanish. Moipa slumps back in his chair, satisfied that his people will be paid. Primo is exploitative, which conflicts with my own hypocrisies, but I would follow Moipa to the ends of the jungle. But clearly, I should have paid my full fare.

The road finally takes us to a creek with a slight rainbow sheen on the surface. Our dugout canoe is parked underneath a narrow wooden bridge at this modest feeder stream. The motor is gassed, the boys are excited, and the girls are fearful.

The dugout is surprisingly spacious. We load the canoe with our little chicken cage, complete with chicken.

We set the firewood and food at the back of the dugout and throw our packs up front, cautiously balanced, lest we take a nose dive and chart a new route to the bottom.

Our guides finish final preparations for our departure. Primo confirms the details on our return trip with the Jeep driver. We need to be sure someone picks us up in five days when we get out of the jungle.

"Todos adentro!" shouts Primo, all aboard! It is time to enter the canoe and venture into an unknown wonderland, lush, vibrant and mysterious.

Moipa hands out the long poles that he gathered, so we can all slowly push ourselves away from the creek banks. After navigating the dead, mossy trees that litter the river, we lift our sticks and lower the motor. Moipa pulls the ripcord until the motor utters a sputter, sputter, vroom! We proceed slowly until the mellow current propels us into the tributary's grasp.

Hours pass, until the backwaters turn into the mainstream. We all meditate to the sound of the motor and the passing of the environment. The soft purr of the motor drowns out the occasional slosh of water against the hollow tree in which we all now float.

The sweet smell of the world's freshest air permeates our senses. The towering trees combine with the power of the river flowing beneath our canoe, reminding us that Mother Earth is in charge here.

Moipa guides the dugout to the earthen banks of the river and we all disembark onto the shore. The rainforest wood is far too wet to start a fire, but thankfully Moipa brought along a camp stove from Coca, which allows us to fry some eggs. We set up our tents, we sleep here tonight. The guides are staying together, the girls are staying together, and I guess I'm bunking with Diego.

Our campsite is sandwiched between the river and a wall of greenery that is waiting to be penetrated. Primo hands us the machetes and we began hacking the vines.

The wall of green quickly becomes a doorway and we all step through. With me in the lead, the pace of our excursion depends solely on the speed of my machete. The jungle wall opens even further, revealing the wild boar trails and a path only lightly trodden.

Day Two

We are in Moipa's territory. He is from here, but I'm not sure exactly sure where here *is*. I see only mud, trees, and some scurrying little animals. We feel the moisture on our skin and hear exotic birds cawing in the trees, while the air drips warm tears on our rain gear.

Moipa stops the group to show us some of the jungle's secrets. He grabs a shelled nut that has fallen from a nearby tree, holds it to his mouth, and blows. It sounds like a melodious police whistle, low and oaky. He advises that should we separate, we need to find a nut and repeat what he just did. Moipa will hear it and come save us. He then takes a rock, brakes open the shell, and eats the nut contained within.

Several Howler monkeys pass above us in procession, swinging like mini Tarzans in the overhead canopy. We find our own vines that sweep across the open floor, and we copy the monkeys. We continue to play while our leaders plan our next adventures.

A cool breeze parts the trees, allowing the sun to peep through the holes in the canopy. The sun stays only long enough to remind us that it is out there, and then the curtains close again. This land is basking in shadow. It is a perpetual dusk at its most romantic height. The muted light sheds a surrealistic hue that highlights the already brilliant green and red foliage.

"Are you thirsty?" asks Moipa. We all agree that water would be nice, but our site is too far, and the nearest Quickie Mart is about a week away. He leads us to a nearby tree and hacks off a thick vine at about mouth level. Drip. Drip. Drip. Out comes enough liquid to wet our tongues and swish a bit. When done, Moipa smears dirt where he cut the vine to seal the wound and stop the trickle of water.

Moipa leads us to another tree. With our machetes, we take some scrapings from the bark. We gather large jungle leaves and tie them with thin vines to construct a funnel, or more accurately, a filter. Moipa props it up with sticks, and we put the bark shreds into the filter and saturate it with rain water. It comes out the other end of the funnel in the texture of snot.

Moipa teaches us how to make poison for hunting. The bark would be cooked over the fire and concentrated like a fine-wine reduction until it becomes creamy and lethal. It goes on the angry end of a dart that will be shot into the bloodstream of a monkey. Then it takes the monkey about fifteen minutes until the it falls dead out of the tree. It is important for me to learn how to gather food, just in case I get lost and can't find a nut-whistle.

These are not our lands, we will not shoot monkeys, but the two guides decide to provide us with a vivid theatric portrayal. Demonstrating the hunter-monkey relationship, they chase each other around the tent. These two guides are opposites, but they find common ground outside of civility.

The sun begins to fade from the dim canopy glow and we unpack the firewood from the dugout. This wood is reserved for nighttime conversations and protection against the spirits of the forest. The campfire is our human way of marking our territory, keeping out the curious creatures of the night.

Diego, Moipa and I take frequent walks, while Primo mostly talks to the Chilean girls back at camp. We like to explore our surroundings and learn everything that Moipa can teach us.

Moipa digs up a root from the forest floor and says "se llama anesthesia." We chew it and our mouths go numb. Against Moipa's recommendation, I grind some of the root and roll it in with my tobacco.

We come upon a rotten log that is slowly sinking into the damp ground. There is a steady stream of ants crusading across some leaves and descending into a hole in the log. Moipa takes a leaf, scoops up about twenty ants and eats them. "Taste like lemon," he says. "Try." I do. He is right. Moving on.

Moipa shows us the land, the trees, what to eat and how not to die. He is the expert on plants, roots and all neat nature things. He bends over to pick up some mushrooms.

"Ayahuasca," he says, holding the stem. He points to his head and says "Bueno para las visions." It has helped the Hourani people connect to the spirit world for centuries, maybe millennia. Ayahuasca is a hallucinogenic concoction reserved for life's most transcendent occasions. It requires the mushrooms we just gathered, mixed with the vines that Moipa is now showing us. "Three days," Moipa says in Spanish.

"Que?" I respond in surprise, running the itinerary through my mind. We only have four days left in the jungle. I look back at Moipa, he is waving his finger at nose-level, saying "No!" Instead, we take the shrooms back to camp and make a tea that tastes like Earth.

Moipa's tribe prepares Ayahuasca by turning the mixture into a powder using the influence of fire and water, then further process it until it is congealed into a small gooey ball, much like the poison we just made from tree bark. The little ball goes into the end of a long hollow stick. The recipient tilts his head back and holds the stick to his nose. The mixture is then shot straight into the naval cavity at high velocity.

As Moipa tells this story, I picture myself being at the other end of this tube, hands supporting the trajectory straight to my brain, awaiting an hallucinogenic projectile. This scares me. I thought Ayahuasca was a drink or something to smoke. I'm relieved that we are not going to shoot balls of jungle drugs up our noses. *Although if we had more time...*

A toucan bellows. The EE-OO of a monkey's call chases the wind. The forest walls are immense, like an airplane hangar, while the wildlife is testing the acoustics like a handful of flute players perched in the rafters. The campfire crackles and melts away the condensation the wood acquired throughout the rainy day. The fire casts its flickering shadow on the tents behind us. The moon glow complements the ambiance, silhouetting the canoe and bouncing its reflection off the water in front of us. We climb into our tents and fall into the first sleep since Baños and the deepest sleep I can remember.

Day Three

The morning sun breaks through the canopy. Primo cooks oatmeal while we load our supplies back into our dugout. After breakfast, we push off from the bank, lower our motor, and meander down-river. The deeper we get into the jungle, the closer we get to the village.

We continue for five hours, when we start to hear sputters from our motor. We check the gas, it's fine, but the propeller won't spin! The last little oomph from our outboard engine is used to reach the river banks. It breathes its last breath and dies.

Everything is quiet. Our two leaders are showing their first signs of fear. Frustrated, they jump out into the knee-high mud, scour the banks, and find two long sticks to push us through the water again. The river bottom is a few meters down and the mud is thick. Our sticks gush and slurp as we attempt to propel ourselves forward. We need more robust sticks.

I feel like royalty being serenaded through the Venice canals, resolute to enjoy the environs, until Primo enlists my help. He's tired, and rightly so. It is time for Diego and I to earn our keep.

We have four days before we need to meet the Jeep at the bridge, so we push further down the river. We float for half the day until we come to a dangerous realization. All hopes of reaching the Hourani tribe have now been replaced with the concern that we won't make it back to the Jeep in time, if at all.

We assess the situation and agree on a new itinerary. We cannot make it all the way to the village, there are too many unknowns. We must turn around. We are up a creek without a paddle, a stick, an engine or anything else that might propel us home.

After motoring straight down-river for the last few days, it would likely take weeks to push ourselves back to our starting bridge. If we continue onward with the river flow, we risk exhaustion and starvation when we try to get out of the jungle. Our Jeep driver would need to call a search and rescue party before we ran out of food, batteries, propane, and hope.

The mood has turned solemn. Moipa and Primo embrace the fact they might have to work harder than ever without the luxury of mechanical propulsion. Diego and I assure them that we are all in this together and we will help push. The girls don't offer to help though, they are in their own bubble, huddled. Diego kneels in the back of the dugout and I sit up front, each on our opposing sides. Our sticks push us through the sludge.

The jungle is as vast as any ocean. As the sea swallow's sailors, thus does the jungle swallow the unaware traveler. Fallen trees float past our canoe in succession. On one log, a precariously perched turtle sits with his head telescoping towards our boat. His head droops low to skim insects from the top of the river.

This turtle is completely unaware that on the other side of the planet, millions of people are scurrying to get to work or calling their spouses to tell them they will be late for dinner. In this place, time has no immediate influence. It merely passes by on the river of life like a turtle on a log.

The seasonal floods have just begun. The water is high. We push some more and hug the shore. Exhausted and hopeless, we bank our boat to rest on a muddy beach framed by leafy trees.

At the other end of the beach, an iridescent blue butterfly hovers above something small, white, and conspicuous. I approach cautiously. Is this an animal, is it poisonous? Did something wash ashore from the river? If this is a stone, it is eerily out of place in the mud. I poke it with my stick and approach closer. Bending down a few feet from it, I can't help but feel both humor and disgust. I giggle and call Diego over to take a look.

We are not the first people to land on this beach. Someone stopped here within the last few days to take a shit on this beach and they didn't bury their toilet paper!

We sit on the banks in quiet contemplation when we hear a low, quiet hum coming from down-river. Our guide's ears perk up like guard dogs.

The Hourani tribe have strict regulations about how many people can visit their park and their homes. We are supposed to be the only boat on this river, but around the corner, thankfully, another canoe comes into view!

This dugout is identical to ours, like a mirrored reflection on the surface of the water. It is packed with eight visitors and two guides - twice our numbers. They are all just as muddy as we are. Ten people and all their supplies is a tight fit in one canoe, but for some grace of god, they are also carrying a second motor!

How fortuitous of them to think ahead for us! We have one motor that doesn't work and they have two that function fine. The solution seems obvious, but they still have two days' journey to get out of the jungle. We would be leaving them vulnerable if they give us a motor and their primary motor dies.

"If we come back in three days and you're still here, we will give it back to you!" I shout, mostly joking, but with a twinge of desperation in my voice. They laugh.

They seem benevolently eager to help us. Primo cajoles the other guides and convinces them to swap our shitty little stove and upgrade our wet gear! It seems we booked the bargain safari, but with the help of the first-classers, the despair drifts away and hope revives the laughter. We've made friends, however temporary.

"You guys good?"

"Same as you now, I presume!"

They tell us a parting story about the anaconda that swam under their boat, and where to beware. Their guide starts the motor and roars up the river, waving kind salutations until they disappear around the corner.

We take a minute to adjust our new gear, and then resume our trip in the opposite direction, away from our saviors, floating down the river in style. We can still go to the village now!

We've lost almost a full day since we've been on this unplanned detour paddling around in circles. We cruise straight down the river without delay. We only slow down to avoid the floating logs. We must hurry.

Night falls. We set up camp on the driest and most secluded beach we can find. Primo wants to camp on the other side of the river, but Moipa talks him out of it, saying something about tribal boundaries.

The tents are pitched, and the canoe is unpacked upon the banks. We are intent to go back out on the river to explore in darkness. Our new motor works, but we don't want the obscene noise to disturb the pristine or scare the animals away. We push with our sticks to maintain our cloak, although I'm sure the entire animal kingdom knows we are here.

The occasional twitter of a songbird echoes off the forest walls, playing tricks on our senses. The night is made eerie by the moon shining through an obscure window in the corner of the forest hangar. The rainforest proves to be its own self-contained supermarket, but the difficulty is in learning how to shop here. Food is abundant, water is available, and recreation is plentiful.

"You know caimanes?" Primo asks. I look at Diego, we look at the girls. Everyone is confused.

"No," Diego responds. "Who is that?"

"Not *who* - what!" Primo responds with a giggle. "They are like crocodiles, small alligators, about this big," he says, fully extending his arms. "They are in the water. Do you want to find one?"

Diego and I instantly agree while the two Chilean girls are significantly more hesitant. We postulate that they stay behind in their tents, on this lonely beach, with other foreign animals lurking in the trees. They quickly change their minds and board the canoe.

We are caiman hunting. The forest air is calm but slowly breathing. The water is still. Primo guides us to the river equivalent of a dark alley, but he takes us too close to the banks. The tributary is barely five meters across, and the moss-covered vines reach out to touch the water like the trunks of a herd of elephants drinking.

We stray under the creepy overhanging growth. Snakes are designed to blend into these surroundings, spiders are virtually invisible, and I wonder what other man-eating creatures live here.

As we slowly float, Primo kneels at the bow shining his flashlight into the swampy growth where the water meets the bank. He is waiting for eyes to shine back at us. We spot two glowing orbs through the darkness. Primo keeps his light fixed on our reptilian prey as the boat glides closer. Moipa reaches down.

When shining a flashlight in a caiman's eyes, they become as docile as deer. He quickly grabs the creature by the neck and snout, acutely aware it will put up a fight for its life once the caiman realizes what's happening. Moipa muzzles the beast with his gloved hand and presses the miniature dragon close to his body.

Shining for caiman isn't real hunting though. The Hourani don't use flashlights, that's cheating. They hunt caiman to feed their families, but we will do no such thing. We still have oatmeal. We return the caiman to its habitat, primed for some young tribesman to later catch for a meal or to prove to his tribe that he is worthy to become a man.

Day Four | December 25th

A Toucan's squawk wakes us at dawn with the sun. It is morning in the jungle and today we visit the village. The dim glow of the canopy light washes away the night. I walk down and sit on the banks to write in my journal, this very journal, when five small Hourani children cautiously peer through the trees. I smile at them, they come out slowly and surround me.

They giggle amongst themselves. One boy reaches out to touch my long blonde braid. After seeing that I will not bark or bite, the rest of the children approach to see what madness this blondeness is. I feel mostly appreciated, but there is an awkwardness about this.

One little boy has twelve toes, he is my favorite. He won't stop smiling and that makes me smile too. Of all the children, he is the most obsessed with my hair, but I am also entranced by his unique feet. He has no sandals, and no shirt, he is only wearing a pair of old, blue gym shorts. His round happy face matches his round brown belly. We have hand-gesture discussions for the next twenty minutes until Primo interrupts the cultural exchange.

"Pack camp!" Primo shouts from his post at the stove. My new friends are startled like their parents were calling them home. The little boy tries to get me to follow them, but Primo shoos them away. We have work to do. All five of the children jump into the river and start swimming away!

The Hourani expected us to arrive yesterday, but our motor has caused delays. We push off to make the final leg to the village. After pushing off, we putter around a corner, into the cove, to see the five children having a splash fight. We're already here! We camped only minutes from their beach. We cut our motor and drift calmly to the shoreline and onto the dirt dock.

A dark-skinned elder man greets Primo before we even get out of the boat. The elder is shirtless and his bulging tummy has popped out his belly button. His mullet haircut looks as if it was cut with a sharp rock. His shorts match those of my favorite little twelve-toed boy, and as it turns out, this is his father. Their familiarity is also evident in their constant smiles.

The other men are out hunting, but they'll be back for lunch. The dirt track has two thatched huts on each side and a larger hut in the back. The walls are strong but absent of windows. Five women gather in a circle in front of one of the huts, chatting. I would love to know what they are talking about. Do they gossip, do they discuss sports, are they trading weaving ideas? I will never know.

The kids exit the water and ask to play soccer with us. Their ball is flat, but sadly, we cannot help. We kick the ball back and forth as we walk to the rear hut.

Grandma is sitting in a hammock. Her dark, droopy tits, flat like the soccer ball, are fully exposed in the jungle humidity. She is tending the fire and knitting something, hopefully a shirt for my favorite little boy. He follows me everywhere, chewing on that big leaf that he carries around.

Three men come out of a path hidden by the trees. They pay us little attention, walking right past us to their women folk. The women all let out exasperated sighs when they realize the men are empty handed. The hunt didn't go well.

There is a skinned monkey hanging from the eaves of the hut's open frame. It looks like it was cooked a few days ago, but there are no flies. One of the men tears a leg away and gruffly offers it to me. I decline, but signal with my fingers "just a little piece."

It tastes like the leathery bear I had during my first Alaskan winter, like jerky stuck in my teeth. There is not enough monkey to go around, but we will happily cook lunch and share with the tribe.

We feast on fresh chicken. Our pet has been very well behaved on this trip, never complaining, unlike the Chilean girls. But we can't eat the Chileans, so Moipa uses his machete to end the chicken. The girls are disgusted by our chicken's death, but fortunately Moipa was holding its legs before he chopped off its head. This prevents it from running blind and brainless.

Primo is a decent cook. He de-feathers the chicken and guts it. He puts the entrails in a bucket and puts the filets aside for the fire. Our avian traveling companion goes into the pot with some of our potatoes and rice. Moipa throws some weird leaves in with it. I keep a close eye on him, making sure he doesn't sneak other strange things into our meal. I trust him, but everyone likes to pull off a good prank when presented with the opportunity.

Today is Christmas, but in the jungle this date has no meaning. The tribe is unaware of what happened two thousand years ago on a different continent. They also do not hold the Christian missionaries in high regard. They only brought weapons and diseases to this land.

New Year's Day is the only Hourani holiday, but that isn't until springtime when the ants get their wings. This starts another cycle. There is no need to heed the imaginary constructs of western calendars. They are impractical to the ants, the locals, and to me in this moment. I just need to watch for the month of March.

After lunch, the happy father goes into his hut and comes out with a thick pole about two meters long, slung across his shoulder. It looks like bamboo, but it is incredibly dense and hefty. This is his blow-dart gun. Around his other shoulder hangs a string, tied to a shiny black seed half the size of a coconut. It appears to emanate fluffy white cotton, whisping out of a hole in the top. He pulls a quill from his bamboo quiver and wraps the tip in cotton. He inserts the newly formed dart into the end of his pole, raises it to his mouth, and sounds a "Pfoo!"

The dart impales a banana on a tree twenty-feet away. We aren't using the poison we made yesterday, the banana will live. We take turns shooting at the banana, but I really just want to see if I can hit a monkey.

It is time for us to go. The kids come to give us hugs and say goodbye. I awkwardly shake hands with the father, and wave to the women who don't wave back. I nod at grandma and she nods back. It will be a day and half against the current until we get back to the bridge where I hope our Jeep will be waiting for us.

Day Five | Forest Farewell

We leave the village and set out to fish for pirañas. Twenty minutes upstream, we find an inlet cove and park the boat. The banks are steep, like the earth melted away, exposing the bare nerves of the trees and mud. The water is murky but calm, with a thin layer of bugs hovering on top. We get out and crawl up the steep incline, using the roots to assist us.

Primo follows behind us, carrying the bucket of chicken guts he saved from the lunchtime butchery. He passes out a few hooks and some fishing line wrapped sticks. Moipa ties his hook to the line and baits it with a small piece of intestine from our chicken friend.

Moipa kneels, looking over the edge of the bank. "Mira, watch." He tosses his hook into the water, drags it for a few seconds and pulls it back up. He repeats four times and seems confused why he didn't catch anything.

Primo grabs his bucket and scoops out some of the blood that has formed little puddles throughout the guts. He splashes the blood into the water to excite the fish.

Baby pirañas nip at the surface, cresting the water like tiny little dolphins. The smaller ones are translucent, opulent, appearing white as they breach the surface. Their tiny razor-sharp teeth nip at the air as they came rushing up through the blood. They expect meat, but there is none. Moipa tosses in his hook and snags one on his first try.

The bigger piraña lurk a few inches below the dark water, close enough to see the tips of their dark spines, but they don't come to the surface. Every time I throw my hook in, those pesky translucent bastards attack it and eat my bait before it can sink low enough! If I can get my hook past the little white guys on top, I might catch a bigger one down below. Meanwhile, Moipa has six.

We eat well tonight. After cooking our fish, Moipa carves out a set of piraña teeth for me. I carefully put them into my backpack. I put my head on my pillow and drift asleep to our last night of jungle sound serenades.

When daylight breaks, we hastily pack our canoe and race up the river. We meet our waiting jeep in the early afternoon. We are outbound, heading towards Coca when Moipa asks me, "You happy you're going home?"

This is not our natural habitat, but we have become intimate with these surroundings. This place invigorates even the heartiest of city dwellers, but we cannot remain here. Visions of the green cathedral ceilings pass through my mind, and then the oil plume, billowing smoke into the sky, comes back into view.

Nature has embraced me in her bosom, revealing her vulnerabilities. She can help us survive if we listen. I hear leaves rustling in the breeze, the water splashing against the trees, and I respond somberly, "No. I'd rather stay here."

Shared Visions

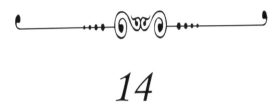

14

I am in Quito, back at the spiky fence, staring at the shards of broken glass that protect our small blue schoolhouse. The classmates have changed. My Cotopaxi partner, Carlos, has disappeared down the mountain range, and the jungle crew has dispersed. I am back where I started. I am weathered, but I am home.

It's been a week since I left for Baños, and I now realize I never told the school I was going into the jungle. I wonder if Jimi notified them that my weekend trip to Baños was extended. By the look on my teacher's face, she did not. I should have told someone where I was going, but at the time, I didn't even know.

I've been here for two months and I've grown comfortable. I know my way around the land and the people, but it is time to become anonymous again. It's time for me to go. It is time to leave Jimena behind and go drink mescaline. I break the news to Jimena that the time has come, and I talk to the school. I am leaving on New Year's Day - which is tomorrow.

Its New Year's Eve and hundreds of people march through the streets, many with parade floats and ten-foot dolls, yet it is a sober and somber evening for Jimena and me. We embrace, lean next to a light pole, and watch the ebb of life flow around us.

After the procession, we stroll back to her house to make our own dolls. We stuff jeans and old shirts with crumpled newspapers and stitch a scary head on top of a discarded T-shirt. We grab matches and lighter fluid, and then exit her house onto the street.

Burning these dolls symbolizes a rebirth, the passing of an entire year, washing away our sins to start clean again. It is the end of my Spanish studies and time to leave the friends I have met. It is the end of my time in Quito and most painfully, the end of my time with Jimi.

Week Eight | *January 1*

I head south, down the continent's spine towards Peru. Thousands of kilometers still lay ahead before I will arrive at Machu Pichu, but I must first get out of Ecuador. I could take the Pan-American Highway and be in Lima on a 30-hour bus. No, that's not right, I'm not in a hurry.

Eleven hours down a different route, away from the highway, nestled in the Valley of Longevity, there is a small mountain village called Vilcabamba. Its inhabitants are rumored to live to be 130 years old! This valley is also the best location to find the San Pedro mescaline cactus. I must discover if this is a coincidence - or if there's a connection between this hallucinogen and everlasting life. I'm going to Vilcabamba to enhance my immortality.

The trip south through Ecuador requires a few stops. Firstly, there's an overnight stay in Cuenca, and one more stop in Loja before continuing to Vilcabamba.

Ecuador has been inexpensive, I've spent $1,500 across the last two months. Amazingly, I adhered to my $25 per day allowance. I still have $3,000 before I need to be in Lima to catch the plane back to Seattle. I have both time and cash. A night in Cuenca is a welcome layover.

Upon arrival, of course, I discover that the city of Cuenca is in the middle of her Founding celebrations. I review my guidebook and find the hostel that is "the perfect place for the perfect price."

I walk into the lobby. The desk is located at the corner of a chic café. There are six or eight wooden tables scattered around the concrete floor, leading out to a grassy lawn, with two other cabins visible in the backdrop. At the end of the room there is a plywood stage, where a band plays slow house music.

To stage right, a rock-climbing wall stretches four meters high, with a small group of rugged men trying to ascend. To stage left, there is a door leading to a separate room. The hotel man tells me that is my room and hands me the key. I hit three chairs with my pack as I awkwardly navigate to my door. I open it, stash my stuff, and immediately return to the bar for a drink.

A woman approaches my table and introduces herself as Monika from Berlin. She has pale skin and tightly-trimmed brown hair. She has a perfect complexion with an old-soul smile. She is dressed in the garb of travelers: jeans and a T-shirt. She is a distraction that enables the memories of Jimi's Quito to drift into history.

The vibrations of the universe have put Monika and me together, at this table, thousands of miles from our homelands. She sends me quivers when I hear her speak my native English. I'm a sucker for accents, it's a sign of intelligence to speak multiple languages, no?

We get accustomed to one another over the next three hours, while many other people come to our table just to be friendly. "Where you from? Where you going? Where you been?" It is the default conversation starter when searching for common ground. I'm looking for a new crew to join me in Vilcabamba, on the route to Peru.

I learn that Mathew from Belgium needs to meet his girlfriend for three weeks in Columbia before he goes south to Peru. Jamie and Sara are going straight to Peru in five days. Then, I meet Robert and Nini. They're going to Vilcabamba tomorrow!

Robert is a tall, thin, man in his fifties, with a mustache and thick glasses. He is from Boston. He's a tall, skinny man with a baseball cap and a thick accent. Nini is from Israel. He's younger than Robert. He's always smiling and talking funny. Nini and Robert met in Guayaquil just a few days ago. I think they're lovers.

Monika and I share a hostel room, we have chemistry, but we remain respectfully separate. It's as if we shared a past life, and during that life there was an intense battle that we barely escaped. We are two samurais saluting each other during the changing of the guard. She is traveling north to Quito and I am still heading south. We are resolute that our paths will end here in Cuenca. But there is still the question of 'when'. I will not be catching that bus tomorrow morning. Monika and I have plans.

I am either simply unable to resist distractions, or I'm way too slow to pack. It's been three days since I met Monika, but we are only now saying goodbye. I board the bus that goes to Loja and then on to Vilcabamba. By evening, the bus stops at the central plaza in the Valley of Longevity. This scene could be featured in an old western movie. It's a quaint, dusty town made from wooden buildings. It has a nostalgic and familiar peace about it. It reminds me of home, with smooth rolling hills, sheep in the green pastures, and a little river running east of town.

Pachamama is the most popular hostel in the region. It is Quechua for Mother Earth. It is also where I am supposed to meet with Robert and Nini, but I'm three days late. A taxi takes me up the hill, and as soon as I arrive, I feel like I am home.

The main cabin serves as a gateway for when visitors first arrive. A handful of trails emanate from here, leading through the shrubs to a myriad of little cabins sprinkled around the hillside.

The cabins are little more than four walls and a roof. They are just wide enough for a pair of wooden bunk beds on each side of the entry way. It's a blend between an outhouse and a jail cell, with the aroma of fresh wilderness and isolation.

The feeling is familiar, but the faces have changed. The vibes, the resonating energy, the thrill of the country, the excitement of youth and this thrill of the unknown has become normal.

I see Robert and Nini sitting on the central patio leading to the courtyard. I feel like I either missed the movie or I am early for the next one. Robert is leaving for Panama and Nini is heading to the Galapagos. They check out of Pachamama just as I check in.

I enter my room and meet yet another German girl named Diana. She is sitting on her bed in her underwear reading a book. She is my new roommate, but sadly, she is leaving tomorrow morning. We stay up laughing and talking until the morning hours. We make plans to meet in Chiclayo, Peru, but distractions will never allow this to happen. I awake in the morning to a gentle kiss on my cheek, and Diana disappears into the world.

I have just missed a tsunami of travelers. Everyone I meet says they have been here for the last few days and are now moving on. I spent too much time in Cuenca and missed the party. It is now the next iteration. I join in passing, through this vortex on its cyclic breath, the next wind, the next wave. Pachamama and mescaline will consume me and then exhale me anew.

After an exploratory hike today, I returned to find that two new Dutch girls have moved into my room. They are both tall, slender, and blonde. All three of us have muddy clothes, hiking boots, and long, blonde hair braided down to our shoulders. We match.

The Amster-dames both jump into alert when I enter their sanctuary through the creaky wooden door. Default discussions ensure, we exchange names and I attempt to enter and set my pack on my bunk.

I duck my head under the door frame and hit Myra with my pack. There is an unwritten rule at these hostels: you will not be guaranteed your own room unless you pay for the entire occupancy of that room. If I keep getting shacked up with lovely European girls, I will continue to enjoy this custom.

"Hello."

"Hi."

"Let's go find hallucinogenic cactus."

We all know why we are in this town. There are two reasons to travel to Vilcabamba, Ecuador: hiking and mescaline, possibly a third reason if you're seeking immortality. I become instant friends with my new roommates. Myra and I will blossom into each other's stories across multiple continents in the coming years.

Pachamama has a pool in the front yard that overlooks the valley. The brown picket fence is only high enough to provide a boundary, I step right over it. In the corner hangs a hammock, and in that hammock swings

Paul. He's a skinny English man. Like me, he is halfway through his twenties. Paul looks like he could have been a Beatle. He has the traditional short dark hair, English cheek bones, high eyebrows, and brilliant accent.

Lon and Lotten are two best friends from Sweden who could double as sisters. They sit next to Paul and giggle. They are young and cute, but they weren't sure if they are ready to go to college. They've come here to explore the alternative education of the world herself, rather than pursuing the indoctrinated scholastics of those who actually run the world. This is a wise life choice; worse decisions have been made. The Swedes just graduated high school and are here to explore nature and culture, but they are not here to explore the inner wildernesses of their minds like we are.

Fran is also from England but lives in Sydney. She is only a few years older than me but has managed to make a home in a foreign country. I need to investigate how I might apply this to my own existence. Fran has wiry red hair that seems to fear brushes. Her pasty skin and freckles don't make her unattractive, but they don't add beauty either. Fran and I will also be intertwined over the next ten years across three continents, but different continents than Myra, and never at the same time.

Matteo is from Switzerland. He looks out of place and uncomfortable, but maybe he's just shy. His English is quite good, but this seems to be true with Europeans.

Mateo is about forty years old, but everyone should be allowed to search for their souls if they must. He is like our cool uncle, but he can relate. He is sitting on a stool between the hammock and the pool, trying to become part of the conversation between British Paul and the Swedish Sisters.

Most of us are going for a hike today with the intent of finding the San Pedro mescaline cactus. The Swedish sisters diverge from our quest for illicits. They are not here for the nectar of the Earth. Instead, they wander the hillsides in search of rivers, animals, and other natural beauties. We will all meet again tonight, surrounding this hammock by the pool, but our states will be altered and our delights assured.

Incan shamans have been cooking San Pedro mescaline for three millennia. They believe the juice of the cactus gives you the keys to heaven. God hid them somewhere and this cactus knows where to find them.

San Pedro is also said to make closed minds open and stable minds go crazy. Entire cultures and communities have been built around their visions. Shamans use its teachings to mold their principles and practices. It is one of four holy plants, along with Coca, Tobacco, and Ayahuasca, although according to Moipa, Ayahuasca is a cocktail of many different plants.

San Pedro has the psychoactive properties of the more familiar Peyote cactus but amplified. It is a sacred medicine to purge negative energies. Once immersed, you may find yourself in a dream, with the ability to leave your body and travel freely to other realms. Of course, I don't know all of this yet. I'm just following Paul's lead.

We lace our boots and throw on our packs. We meander along a curvy dirt road towards the town in the valley below. After about six miles, we start seeing what looks like the plant we seek. Mateo finally jumps into action. He hasn't spoken since we left the house, but he points and loudly announces, "Yes, this is it!"

Paul examines his plant book and agrees that this is indeed San Pedro. We look around us and see the tall stalks scattered sparsely throughout the hill. They poke their heads out from the earthen, yellow fields.

"It takes an arm's length to make one dose," Mateo instructs. He seems to know a great deal about harvesting this plant. We know nothing. We begin cutting our stalks to the prescribed lengths. The pricks protect them, they are the size of small needles that could easily pierce our skin. As with society, the pricks must go first. Once the pricks are plucked, Mateo shows us how to peel the layers to get down to the dark green psychoactive cactus meat.

Once the needles are removed, the husk is like plastic. All the cactus juice is concentrated just under the thick skin. Peeling back this protective layer, the soft insides of dark meet lies directly underneath the skin. There is only a small ring of dark green, then it turns into the white core which provides no hallucinogenic favors. We fillet the stalks and fill our plastic bags full of chopped cactus trunks. We bury the remains of the cacti on the hillside in hopes they will sprout again into newborns.

Paul, Myra, Mateo, and I walk through the town center and sit against the stone fountain. We hear a referee's whistle blow in the near distance. "Oh shit, it's the San Pedro Cactus Police!" We look around nervously while our paranoid brains try to make sense.

Paul has seen this before and explains it to us: "The whistle is from a sentry, hired to guard the village. The people pay him to keep watch over the town and give peace of mind to the locals. The people want to be sure the job is done. The last guy was caught sleeping. Now he must keep blowing his whistle so they know where he is."

It seems a quick and efficient fix to a simple problem! Then we realize he is also announcing his position to the bad guys every time he toots his whistle. I wonder if we're the bad guys in this scenario.

Some local guy named Pico usually prepares this mescaline cocktail for the travelers. I heard whispers of Pico when I was at the bus station in Loja. He's the cook, he's the teacher, he's the guide through the nether. He knows what we need and where to go. Unfortunately, Pico was arrested two weeks ago. We're on our own until the universe sends help. Luckily, that will only be a few hours from now.

We met Amanda at the market last night. She is five years older than the rest of us, clothed in torn jeans and an alpaca shawl. Her dirty blonde hair blends into the shawl's patterns. She is the link between the local and the traveler. She bridges these two worlds. She is Canadian, yet nearly native. We are lucky to have met her yesterday, but we are even more fortunate to meet her again just now, coming through the town square, while we sit with our skins in our bags not sure what to do next.

Amanda sees the stalks poking out of our bags, and asks, "Do you guys know what you're doing?"

"Not really," we all shamelessly agree.

"Let me see," she asks. The legality of this drug is not very clear, and I'm also not sure how the Incan culture feels about us chopping down one of their four most sacred plants. Amanda is safe though. We show her the produce and she approves of our work.

"Do you know what to do now? I can guide, I have a house and batch cooking." Amanda has everything we seek. "Hey, you can come, too. It's almost done boiling down. I just came into town for some quick supplies, it's lucky we met." I'll say.

"Do you need these?" I ask, lifting the bag of stalks.

"Sure, we can use them for the next batch." Amanda leads us out of the town square, in the opposite direction, further away from our lodging. We hike for forty-five minutes along a dirt road that threads between the hills. The town fades away behind us and the surroundings are now forests.

Fallen trees line the dirt pathway down a slight slope, past the fire pit, to the wooden porch of the rustic two-story cabin. Amanda's house blends well with the old-growth forest, seemingly made from these same materials, perhaps when it was just a young-growth forest.

The walls are unpainted lumber, caked with dried mud. A harvest of cactus stalks is propped on the side of the house. The kitchen looks like an afterthought, attached to the side of the house on the ground floor. It doesn't blend in with the rest of the house. There is a propane camp stove on the table, just robust enough to boil water for a few hours and maybe cook some eggs if we are still alive in the morning.

The interior is barren and dusty. Lanterns illuminate the dark corners and cast shadows across the wooden floors. The wide balcony on the second floor underscores the large barn windows, none of which have glass. Overlooking the jungle's edge, my mind wanders into the Amazon basin below.

It is a long process to prepare San Pedro but it doesn't take three full days like Ayahuasca. The skins are boiled with a handful of other herbs for about eight hours. This reduces the green meat into a concentrate. I've seen this process before. It is just like the Hourani monkey poison or Big Al's fine wine reductions.

We arrive at Amanda's house at 3:55 pm and we ingest a shot of San Pedro concentrate before the clock strikes 4 pm. Amanda and her crew have spent the day preparing for the night, and we've just come at the climax.

Amanda is our hostess, but she isn't drinking cactus tonight. She hands us each a shot glass. "You can meet our people after you drink this." The juice looks like honey, but it tastes like the devil's piss. We might as well have been reducing vinegar for the last twelve hours.

Amanda then takes us to the firepit. We have an hour to get to know one another before we all accept the keys to heaven and step through the gateway.

A woman approaches and takes the shot glasses from us. "I'm Red," she says. "I'm from Sydney." She won't take her shot tonight either, but instead she'll chew coca leaves all night. We watch in disbelief at the speed at which she cleans the dishes.

"Aye, I'm Ben. I'm with Red." They came here from Australia together. Ben helped cook all day while Amanda was out for supplies, which eventually brought the three of us back here with to arrive in this moment. Ben is 23 years old with long blonde hair and a goatee. He's a lot like me, except for the pseudo-beard and the accent. He drank cactus juice every night this week, so he's a little quirky.

"Laurie, welcome," she says in a New York accent, extending her hand. She's an ethnobotanist scholar and a divine beauty. We talk about the origins of Latin and Spanish until the juice takes hold and I wander into the forest. She is leaving with Red and Ben for Peru in the morning. I will make plans to join them but will miss yet another bus.

"I'm Dara, mate, we're happy to have you guys." Dara is Australian but has a home base in India. "It's been eighteen months since I was in Varanasi, and five years since I was in Canada, but here we are in Ecuador!" I am thoroughly confused and ask him again where he is from. "I'm from here and there. I call them all home."

Dara's hair is straight out of the 1970's. His nose is pierced with an inch-long silver tear drop that droops to his lips. It looks like snot hanging down. He has a master's degree in medicine but couldn't get his doctorate because his thesis was too radical. He follows the four million Sadhu in India pilgrimaging to the Kumbha Mela. I have no idea what this means, but Dara convinces me I should go investigate this for myself next year. I will.

"Ike," he says with a stiff nod of his head. He's 50 years old but looks closer to 70. His gray beard matches his mangled hair. His cut-off jean shorts look like they are his only pair, and he wears them without any underwear. He doesn't wear a shirt either, exposing his dark, skinny, and scarred torso. He lives in Columbia and is mostly just a surfer dude, but don't give him no shit, he's scrappy.

Paul, Myra, Mateo and I are getting comfortable, but something is coming. I feel a fire bubbling up from within. For the next thirty minutes, the power intensifies from my gut, through my torso and throughout all my limbs. My core is being tickled, trembling my essence.

Conversations change. We begin to muse more at our connections to the environment than to our relations with one other. We are being pulled into a new perception, one devoid of disapproval.

Like the apex of a roller coaster, kinetically charged to plunge, we enter our purge, popping into our new realities. Fran is first. She stops midsentence, stares at the tree for ten seconds and then affirms, "It's here." Paul is next, and then Myra, each being suddenly jolted from their current context and pulled into something new.

It is my turn. I push through my existence and pop out the other side like I'm crossing the sound barrier. We've only been at Amanda's house for thirty-five minutes, when the time and our minds begin to fold behind us.

Fireflies flicker in the starry night sky, obscuring the boundaries between earth and her heavens. They trace the skies like little comets coming to rest in the grass, like tiny pixies fleeing heaven. Dara shows us one he caught, then releases it back into the wild. We study the fireflies that are floating on the breeze. They glow like headlights, so they won't have mid-air collisions. It is also a warning, humans could easily hurt them. Pixies are fragile.

The moon peaks over the horizon and shows its face. Instantly, the fireflies disappear into the bushes as if their father moon just ushered them all to bed. The man in the moon has eyelashes and he winks at us. The fireflies turn off their butt-lights and disappear for the night.

The Earth spins steadily under our feet. This is an earth induced spiritual retreat. All the answers to the universe are evident, we know how they are connected, how we all are part of that same ribbon.

We consider bottling this essence to take home with us, but we don't have the resources or the time. More importantly, that would be disrespectful. It is critical that this is experienced in the raw, natural world. It should not be removed. It would be an unfair burden to Amanda and also to the spirits of San Pedro. We dismiss these thoughts and return to the present.

An hour ago, Amanda handed us the keys to heaven and we all stepped through the doorway, as prophesized by the ancient Incas. Everything is now perfectly aligned in a vortex of colors - the crowd, the house, the rhythm, the sunset, the forest, the hammock, the food, the fire.

Ten of us form a cohesive chain, each of us breathing the energy around us, sharing in the divine appreciation from these high Andes, to the valley and jungle below. We give praise to Pachamama, our Mother Earth, for she is our guide.

The campfire flames lick at the sky, like an upside-down waterfall, flowing endlessly into the starry ocean, creating the galaxies themselves.

Total chaos of thought is inevitable when the rules of reality are being rewritten. Laura grabs a stick and starts fishing in the middle of a grass field. Dara wades out to his hips in the creek and stands there for an hour, just staring at the ripples. Ike, the 50-year-old Columbian, keeps waving his arms and repeating "The forest is coming too fast!" He eventually goes inside.

The sun is our majesty and it's reigning hot. The music, it's yellow and blue! Our campfire songs take physical form and begin to walk around the logs, tapping each of us on the soul. The trees have faces and the wind's wings brush across our shoulders.

Paul and I look out from the balcony at all the Christmas lights. There are none, but we both see them. Tiny crimson lights circle each of the branches, spiraling down the trunks before they disappear through the roots and into the earth. We are sharing visions while viewing the energy of the forest. I leave Paul on the balcony and wander alone to the frog pond behind the cabin.

The water is flanked by a mud bank and a small grassy area, but this trip is about the trees that surround us. They are the universe's grand sentries, and they are smiling at me through the faces in their leaves. Their arms outstretch to form a net of protection, guarding me from bad spirits.

A frog hops into the pond. I sit at the base of the largest tree and sink into the mud. Leafy limbs reach down and snuggle me in their embrace, helping to hide me from the world. I am connected, I am invisible, I am entranced, I am whole.

I close my eyes, curl up in a ball, and reflect upon the evolutions that have delivered me to heaven's doorway. I flashback to my youth, to the steps that brought me here, to the past that brought me tears, to my search for the truth.

At the day's end, sun fall is near;
silent light fall, night is all you hear.
I journey to the forest, my ritual awaiting.
I taste the body of Christ, divine will abating.

Visions contouring, the time is blurring.
My mind is melting - illusions stirring.
Fog of thoughts and thoughts of not,
the forest is forgetting what she's taught.

Throughout the years, upon deaf ears,
land the lessons that she's cast.
Lend an ear, to hear her tears -
and the voices from the past.

My soul and spirit seem adaptive,
but my brain is my body's captive.
My mind and body will now collapse;
I begin the future unlike the past.

After Embers

15

Year One | Morphosis

I stand at the intersection of this way and that, between here, there, and wherever. Watching Amber's taillights face away down the highway has made me pensive. It has filled me with a sense of both dread and independence.

The quiet forest air absorbs all sound. It is cold, it is dark, and I am alone. I stand in the light rain with my heavy pack and my combat boots. The heavy rains have subsided, but the ground is still wet and squishy.

I leave the highway, cross the ditch, hop over a composting pile and walk straight into the prime camping real-estate of the Chugach Forest. There's a patch of open floor space, slightly less muddy than the rest, moderately guarded by a circle of trees. I wander up and set down my pack. This is what I've been looking for all night! I don't need to pay for a stupid campsite, but admittedly, security from the elements might have been worth the cost of admission to a formal camping location.

I wish I knew more about animal rectal anatomy, not that I'll ever repeat that sentence again. I cannot distinguish the origin of this little brown pile of poop sitting on this rotten log that I have come upon. I figure it is safer to backtrack to avoid any confrontation with Mother Grizzly or her seven cohorts. I walk along the highway for another ten minutes.

The moonlight glow shines overhead, striking down on the old, overgrown forest. The uneven floor doesn't allow me to hike far from the highway, this spot right here will have to do. Sleeping this close to the road also allows the police to find the remains of my body if a bear finds me and eats me. I need to make it through my first Alaskan camping trip alive. I still have plans.

Concealed in the wet moss, I see the silvery side of a stop sign. This can be my bed, it'll keep me from getting wet. I unbury it, throw it down at the base of a tree and sit down on the cold steel with my back against the trunk. I drift asleep amidst fears of homelessness, starvation, and predatory animals.

I wake to the fresh morning sunshine on my cheeks. I slept for either one hour – or six – I can't tell. I've always been against watches, just for the principle of time, but now I wish to rethink that rebellious decision. One can't rebel against time.

I walk out to my new favorite highway and hear a car. The sun is peeking through again, and the forest has given me cosmic energy to revitalizes my steps. I no longer care about time, money, or bears. The path is forward.

The first driver to stop is an old fisherman in a windowless blue van. He has a shaggy beard, slimy overalls and mean eyes. Under normal circumstances, I would consider him suspicious. I am a trained combat soldier, I'll be fine. On the outside and at the core, I am in withdrawal, but I still have a deeply ingrained kill-switch to flip if things turn ugly.

I open the door and climb aboard. He offers a dour grimace, like he isn't fond of hitchhikers, like he is mad at my thumb. In the Alaskan winter, it is customary that motorists pick up hitchhikers for fear that they might freeze to death in the subzero darkness. I am in no such danger, this isn't even the winter season, but the bearded man still drives me an hour closer to Kenai.

Back on the highway, I stick my thumb out at any cars that drive by. A little Volkswagen slows down, pulls over to the shoulder, and reverses to where I am standing. I walk up to her window as she is rolling it down.

"You can't fit in my car. I'm so sorry." She proves her unavailability by pointing in the backseat, saying "See!" It is filled with her belongings. She wishes me luck and drives away. Odd but nice.

A second car stops and it's another fisherman heading to Kenai for the weekend. His eyes are kinder and his demeanor younger than Shaggy Beard. He's much older than I am, but he isn't the bitter old fisherman or misguided by winter morals to pick up hitchers.

"Where you headed?" he asks me.

"South!" I say with a quirky anxiety.

"Well, I 'spose it's either that – or north!" We are a match. I climb aboard.

"Where are *you* going?" I mimic.

"Going ta Homer for the fish derby this weekend."

"What's a fish derby?"

"It's what we do. We fish!" Ok then. "Whoever has the biggest fish Sunday night wins the cash. Size matters here in the largest state of the union."

While Shaggy Beard sat in silent protest for two hours, this new guy is full of Alaskan factoids and good cheer. I learn about glaciers and wildlife, rivers and bridges. I also learn he is anti-modernization anywhere except the big city of Anchorage.

It is acceptable to bring the cities into the modern age, but don't dare tame the Alaskan wild. Most Alaskans think this way, and I am certain I will also learn to love this place as they do.

He drives me to the local grocery store, not as a cruel joke, but rather because I have nowhere else to go. I say goodbye, and step inside the supermarket to ask a few questions and get the lay of the land.

"Which way to the local cannery?" Someone in Spokane told me that I'm supposed to work in a cannery for the summer.

"Which one?" She says. I cock my head to the side and try to retrace my past conversations with Ethan and Amber. We should be doing this together, I never bothered to ask where Ethan was going. I return my attention to the cashier.

"Which one is closest?" I can't remember the name of any canneries whatsoever. I figure any cannery is better than no cannery. It has been a wild 36 hours since I left home. I need to set up the sanctuary of my tent.

"There's one right down the street and they have a tent city." Perfect, she knows what I need! I desperately need to decompress.

I start walking with my thumb out, and a car instantly stops. We travel mere minutes down a long, sloping road and pull off the road. The smooth pavement breaks into gravel and we park between young trees. A chain is stretched across the dirt road, and from it swings a sign that reads:

Pacific Star Cannery
Employees Only Camping

I am not an employee but I aspire to be. That should be good enough. There is plenty of dry, hard, and level ground to pitch my tent. I am finally at the gates of the fishery, my destination. My Valhalla speaks to me as I duck under the chain, pick my patch of turf and lay claim to the land. I consider taking my Felix the Cat acid tab, but then think it best that I wait until I've slept.

At noon, I hear a rustling outside. Two men emerge from their tents and walk the overgrown path to meet their new neighbor. They are past their prime, in their fifties or sixties, and much more storied than my young spirit.

Their rugged gray beards obscure their faces and make them look like brothers. They both wear tattered denim jackets and holy jeans. They smell of piss and campfire, further confirming that they belong in the wild.

They share their breakfast while we chat and sit on their logs. "This is Ed... and I'm Jaybird. We're from Canada, but we been camping here all winter. It's been quiet until you came along. What's your story?"

I hesitate. I evaluate. They are instantly my new favorite people. I am just adapting to this lifestyle, but it is natural to them. This is controlled homelessness, it is freedom from the grid, and it is terrifying. Ed and Jaybird seem trustworthy, although I'm not yet prepared to bare my soul and reveal the history that brought me here.

"I'm here for the fish!" I proclaim, they laugh.

Ed looks at me intently, "Yeah, but what's your story?" He can smell my history, he just knows. Over the next thirty minutes, we discover that we are alike in many ways. We have traveled similar roads and have befriended the same monsters.

I have been without a dollar for weeks now. I peruse the aisles of the market without any real purpose, I am just looking and passing time, just as I do almost every day. I find chocolate. It fits in my pocket, so it is free. The potatoes and noodles can slide into my sleeves, so they are also free. I confess, it is quite difficult to steal more than a day's ration at a time. I must repeat this every day to survive. I recognize all the employee's faces, so they I am certain they are starting to remember mine. I never go through the checkout line, which raises a few eyebrows. I smile, and everyone just goes back to work.

There have been no sirens or lights yet, but if this continues I may find myself driving into another unpleasant crossroad, this time I would be the passenger in police car. I don't need any more drama, I have enough decision points to navigate.

I owe Ed & Jaybird more than I can steal. The chocolate bars are exquisite, but I think these luxuries need to disappear. I can use this pocket space for a few more packets of noodles. We all understand that we are in this together, but the sugar coating has worn off and I realize how easily I can get arrested for my five-finger contributions to the dynamic.

Today I began my normal daily routine as always. First, I check the cannery. No work. Second, I hitch-hike to the store. On the way, an older, friendly Korean man stops to take me up the hill. He asks me, in a thick accent, "You ever work in restaurant?"

"Huh?" It sounds like a random question, but there appears to be an underlying intent. I reflect on my earlier years and school habits, back to the Corps, a time of folklore, tracing the steps that brought me to this moment.

"Yes, I worked at fast food all through high school." I guess I am in a job interview; the next question corrects my course and put me back on track. These things have cosmic timing.

"My name Unko. You want to come washing dishes at restaurant? You can have meal and..." My mind shuts off at the prospect of real food. He doesn't need to persuade me further.

Camping for the last five weeks, my primary source of intake has been potatoes, ramen, and chocolate. The sustenance is not sustainable. It is all just a dream, my mirage from existence. I've been here long enough to remove the drug fog from my brain tunnels and see the light. I need to rebuild. I haven't eaten a decent meal since Amber's house.

"Yes, that would be nice," I tell him. I am mildly fearful that working around food will only hasten this hunger, but I trust in the goodness of this human to give me a meal at the end of the day. I spend the evening washing dishes and sneaking scraps. I scrub as if my next meal depends on it.

A few days pass, and hope begins to return. Each morning, I look towards the instant gratification of work and then food. I'm like a hamster or a monkey, or one of those rats in a maze. Unko has food at the end of each rush, sometimes before. He lets me wash his dishes and I let him feed me. After a week, he offers.

"If you want, we can do room and board, and I pay you?" Unko pauses. "I think you do good."

"Yes!" I am emphatic but humbled. I agree, and he hands me some cash for my first week of scrubbing. I am a step closer to finding substance to fill the void that has consistently plagued me with doubt.

He shows me to the garage where I will be sleeping for the rest of the summer. There is power, I see an outlet! I need to find a music source. Now I can stop hitching between Kenai and Soldotna, and I can stop stealing my food. My summer is now cast.

I run straight to Carrs and buy a 10# bag of potatoes and a case of ramen noodles of all different flavors. The addition of three chocolate bars, a can of tobacco and a half-rack of beer absorb half of my earnings.

I feel like Santa Claus as I traipse into the campsite. "Ed! Jaybird! Where are you!" They aren't around. I make myself at home at their campfire. Boiling water, peeling potatoes, I am preparing to give these guys a feast. They return, rejoice in my choice, and I leave to pack up my tent. I am sleeping at the restaurant tonight.

Year One | *The Fall*

It has been six months since Amber gave me an acid tab and turned her taillights away. Since then, the great unknown has rinsed me fresh. The chemicals have cleared and I can now check myself out of this immersive inpatient rehab. The fresh mountain air fills my veins and washes the pain away. My first sovereign summer is at its end, but I have stockpiled some cash working for Unko. It's time to go home.

I am 22 years old, a homeless veteran and hardcore partier. I still don't know where I fit in, but this latest endeavor to Alaska has felt the sincerest. The Marines couldn't hold me down, college was never my route, and Spokane was unhealthy and dangerous. Alaska is comfortable. Maybe I'll do this again. And again.

Last spring, when I started down that stretch of Kenai highway, I was at the end of my spiral, tumbling through gateways trying to find my gravity. I was broke, both in cash and in spirit, with only a tent, a prayer and a basic understanding of where I left my sanity.

I'm leaving with $2,500 and a seed in my brain that will sprout into my destiny. It is time to move on. The pink has returned to my skin and I have a new sense of purpose with some cold, hard cash in my pocket.

This route home is the exact inverse of the route that took me here. I'll hitchhike back to Anchorage and buy a plane ticket to Seattle. From there, I'll take a bus to Spokane, and then another bus to Walla Walla.

I enter the triangle. I cannot linger. I know where the edges are. I don't need a guide, but I do need a protector. Gavin still lives here, but he's smart enough not to get caught up in the hype that nearly killed me last year. For the next ten days, he's keeps the bad guys away from me, while we go to bars and band practice.

Spokane is clearer now, more so than when Ethan, Amber, and I left in a flurry. They're not in Spokane when I arrive. No one has heard from Ethan or Amber since we all left last spring. We try to connect a few times, but they both eventually fade into memory.

I wonder if my friends will even recognize me. The last time I saw them, I wasn't a proper friend. My demeanor was burning and my personality was the charcoal. I am still made of that same fragile ego that lurks just beneath the surface, but I've escaped the gravity and floated into my own ethos.

Alaska has given back my essence. Like the ebbs of the tides and the opus of mimes, my shattered core has mended. The

The pieces that the Marine Corps stole away, the pieces that were frozen and dipped in acid, and the pieces that went on life support while everyone sped around me. Those pieces are in remission. The cosmos has been kind and put me in a robust state, catching me in mid-free-fall.

The other fragments, those of my psyche that are ingrained into who I am, they cannot be erased from my core, not even the pits of despair can abolish my being. With the burden of pretense gone, I am reacquainted with myself, relieved that no permanent damage has been done.

The Hermit Collapse

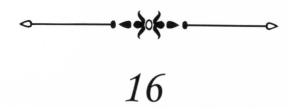

16

I live in a barn. It's my hermit cave, my sanctuary, my studio, and my muse. I sit in the living room and stare at the stockpile of logs outside the window, waiting to feed the antique wood stove. This is my halfway house back to civility after my first Alaskan summer.

The barn is big, old, and sort of sentimental. I spent a few weekends with my family shoveling the cow shit out to turn it into this cabin retreat. We created a cozy 500 square foot apartment with all the essentials – kitchenette with stove and fridge, a bathroom with shower, and a dedicated water tank.

After the Marine Corps, and my downward spiral in Spokane, after mile-marker 223 and other obstacles, I came softly to rest in the place I know best. Home, with mom and dad. For the first time since before the marines, I feel comfortable to be around my family. I still have angst, I am still misplaced, but I am now the closest to my true self that I have ever known. They will let me stay here until I figure things out.

The farm is at the foothills of the Blue Mountains, shielded by tall pine trees and lots of wild grass. The dirt-packed driveway leads first to the barn and my skate ramp. A little further, across the way, is the pathway to my parent's modest farmhouse. The parking area between their house and the barn overlooks a small park area below. Large wooden railroad ties create two paths leading down to the fire pit, the pines, the stream, and the duck pond below.

Walla Walla is where the holes in my soles get mended. It is a small town, funded by onions, wheat, and the state penitentiary. There's a big college here too, which brings in the hipsters from larger cities. Walla Walla is small enough that the generational lines are still clear. Many of our parents know each other from when they were kids.

My mom trains horses and spends her time taking care of lost birds. Dad drives the tractor around and shoots at snakes. They are both newly retired police officers. They still know all the other cops in town, which presents unique scenario when my parties get busted. If the cops don't arrest me, they always tell my parents.

When I saw mom and dad last spring, I could barely look them in the eyes through my junkie filters. I knew I was doing wrong and I knew they would see right through me. This time though, my soldier awkwardness and my addict shame are both gone. I now get to be me – just me.

I spend the days building fence to pay rent and I ride my bike ten miles into town for karate class twice a week. This is my penance for my past sins. I have made a few running attempts at life, only to trip over the hurdles. I will need to find my way back to the forests of Alaska. I'll try again when the winter chill fades, the icicles melt, and the tundra frost thaws.

The hermit life lasts until I come out of hiding for the New Year's party. I connect with scattered with remnants of my teenage years and my skateboard friends. It's only been five years since those days, but these recent years have weighed eternal upon my genesis.

Macy is still here in Walla Walla. We have a sordid and unique history. Our parents both worked together as cops since we were wee tiny tots. We're like each other's evil twins. I didn't see her for ten years after my dad retired, but we got together again in high school and our relationship became exploratory.

Fast forward to now, she's living with me in my parent's barn, and we begin to explore again. We have similar interests, habits, and addictive personalities. These things tend to get me into trouble, particularly when Macy introduces me to Cole.

After the new year's party, I stop biking to karate. I have better things to do. The motivation to kick that gym bag fades and is replaced by an old friend. I got my driver's license suspended in Spokane after those two drunk driving tickets. I can't legally drive, plus I traded the White Rabbit for a bicycle, and then that bicycle got stolen. I'm stuck out here.

The age is eternal, the world is fresh, but we are still stupid enough to get back into the hard stuff. I have been clean for nine months, when I begin to feel that cruel slip of the slope. I like to push limits, but I do fear I've already wandered too close to this edge. It turns hopes into dirt and friends into foes.

I can do this. I can wallow in sweet reverie and not get marooned. But if I dwell too long, I will revel with the devil until I am wholly consumed.

I need to participate. I need the excitement. I need the rush. Some connections and instincts run deep enough to tickle your essence. I am not yet to be confused for a monk but I am in a strong place. I can come out of hiding, my spirit can survive, I won't succumb. Nope, I'm unable to convince myself.

One weekend in March, we went to see the Grateful Dead in Portland. At least I think we did - I remember the parking lot and lots of balloons. When I finally got home, I walked in my parent's house to tell them I was back.

"Your mother needs to talk to you, I can't. Just can't." That's all dad said. Mom enters the living room. There is palpable tension forming in beads upon our foreheads. Something is wrong, I'm not sure how bad I should feel.

I try to read my mother's stone-cold face during the uncomfortable pause that ensues. It can't be about the cops stopping me last spring at mile-marker 223. We already talked about that. Spokane is four hours away and those people don't know where I live, I'm certain they didn't talk to my parents while I was in Alaska. This can't be about anything that just happened at the Grateful Dead show. That's too new, and most of us are too dazed to talk about it anyway.

"What's this about?" I ask.

"This," mom says, with her arms outstretched in front of her. In one hand, she holds my bong. In the other, she holds the wooden box that houses my straws, a razor blade, and a small lightly frosted cosmetic mirror. I am rightfully horrified. I've been discovered, I'm a godless fraud. I'm in relapse and the dream is about to collapse.

My mother presents these items to my face, which is now petrified and paralyzed as I fumble in the darkness for words – any words. Her resolute eyes grab through my soul and capture my spine. I hang my head low and wonder why there aren't more cases of spontaneous human combustion. Now would be a good time to burst into flames.

"We need to talk about this, but we aren't going to do it now," mother says. "I want you to think carefully about how this conversation should go. Good night." She turns her back and walks away, while dad sits in his chair looking out the window.

I saunter out across the grassy parkway and into my apartment. For six hours, I stare at the stack of firewood. I remember chopping that firewood with my dad, as we've done since I was little. I see the bridge across the creek that I helped build a few years ago, before I left for the Marines. Looking even further, I see dear foraging in the pasture, blissfully unaware of life's complexities. I want to be a deer.

After a refreshing summer in Alaska, my skin returned to pink, my teeth stopped rattling in my mouth, and I enjoyed the light. I no longer hid in the shadows. The gravity of the triangle sucked me back into its clutches. I traveled too close.

Something did not stick after my last escape. In Spokane, I narrowly escaped with thirty dollars and a one-way ticket to the tundra, but I did stumble upon something beautiful. This barn relapse will not infect me. But if the poison does reach my heart, and I start to come apart, Alaska has the antidote to cleanse me.

Morning breaks and I awaken under a dark cloud of gloom. I must face my parents and map my future. I walk across the pathway and into their home.

"Sit." I do. A handful of awkward seconds slip through my fingers and drip onto the floor.

"We will pay for your rehab, but you need to stop that shit and stop it immediately." My parents are holding the permission slips for my field trip back to the forest.

My midnight meditation showed me what I need to do.
It's March now, and it's time to go back to Alaska.

   The winter has been gripping, but it only served as
an intermission from admiration. The northern forests are
free from the illicit. They don't have the same temptations.
Last summer was entirely refreshing. It cleansed my pores
and opened my chakras. I need to follow this through and
try again. I need to get back to Alaska. My parents are
convinced, and my path forward is carved. They don't
know that Colin will be coming with me.

   Spokane birthed my wicked psyche and Alaska
tamed it, but as my pet, I still must feed it. My cavalcade
of skeletons marches forward, pushing me into my own
closet. Only I can lead the charge in my mind's composite.

   The path are laden with thorns and spikes, but the
skeletons always crumble. Alaska has the power to fix this,
the power to part the trees and show me the way. I return
and rejuvenate.

Conflicting Beacons

17

I awaken from my trance.
A frog croaks and hops into the pond. I am melding with the earth, sunk in the dirt. I rise, my soul spliced with the tiny red lights spiraling down the tree trunks. I'm revived, summoned to something higher, partnering with the euphoric settings of the Valley of Longevity. I'm connected to the eerie starlight sky, and the rolling hills stretched below. All is one.

A temperate breeze rustles the trees. I am still wrapped in leaves, snuggled like a newborn baby. The protective branches slowly retreat, rising towards the sky, absolving me back to the world, tabula rasa, my spirit true.

If the earth were an orange, San Pedro mescaline would be the fresh-squeezed morning juice, ripe with nutriment. This cactus is coursing through my veins and my brain right now, but my visions are fading.

A half-fallen tree, covered in moss, is wedged at the edge of the pond. My eyes follow the branches until I see Dara squatting up high and watching me. We lock eyes for a moment, and then he darts back to the house without a word.

I rise to my feet. The Christmas lights fade. All the trees, the forest sentries bent over like old men, slowly straighten their spines and stand upright. Their branches like arms align to my passage, clearing the way and sending me back to the campfire. My perspectives are reset. I am newly immortal.

When I first left for the frog pond, Paul was looking over the wooden balcony at the Christmas lights. He is still there, still watching. Laura was fishing in a field, while Dara was knee deep in the creek staring at a bush. They have come back and joined Myra and Fran who are now studying tree bark. I see Ike laying inside the house on the floor. Amanda and Red are huddling in the outdoor kitchen, and Mateo is taking pictures. Wait, what?

Before we started this journey, Amanda went over the rules, reminding us to "give good vibes only, be respectful, and bond with free thought. It's important to be solid. We are all links in the same chain. If you want to take pictures, do it now. There will be no photos from this point forward." That was in the other world though, not here and now.

202

I walk slowly. The earth feels like a mattress and my limbs are made of lead. I approach Fran and Myra, I lean forward and gently ask, "All good?"

Myra turns quickly. "Amanda and Red are worried," she says in her sexy Dutch accent. "How long have you known Mateo?"

Mateo joined us this morning at Hostel Pachamama trying to get involved in our poolside conversations. We're all here for the same reason, but Mateo did not drink the juice. His purpose for joining this trip is in question.

"I met him at the hammock, ten minutes before we left this morning," I assure.

Fran looks up, her worried face surrounds her dilated eyes, twinkling in firelight. Her red hair is matched by the fire's orange hue. "Me too, I just met him. Amanda thinks he's Interpol. He's taking pictures and even asked her for the address."

"What's Interpol?" I try to grasp the situation. We are all birds nesting in the same forest, but Mateo is a worm with a different agenda. We can sense it.

"The International Police," Fran says, intently fixed on my eyes. "And we brought him here."

He joined us this morning to go cut down some stalks. He was with us when we met Amanda in the courtyard, and he's with us now. But the same could be said of any one of us, we're all newly acquainted and on a voyage together. We are nearing the end of our spiritual rebirths and ingesting the peyote of the Andes. Well, not all of us are.

Ben and Ike move out to the fire and sit on a log. They lean towards each other and whisper. Dara is now standing on the other side of the fire, flashing glances towards Mateo who is leaning next to a tree, camera now draped at his side. I find my own log, and stare into the fire, drying off the dampness of the frog pond.

"I think I'm going to go," Mateo startles me. "I didn't drink the juice and everyone is acting cagey."

"Amanda and Red didn't drink either," I tell him, indicating where he could find like minds. This also shuts down any attempt he might make to convince us we are paranoid, and that he wasn't really taking pictures. Red and Amanda saw too.

"They won't talk to me, they seem scared. I think it's the coca leaves." Mateo sounds sincere. I don't want to heighten everyone's fear by questioning him to see if he's an Interpol agent, that doesn't sound fun. My fragile psyche can't handle this discussion right now. I look at his camera and look back at him.

"Do you know the way home?"

"I'll find it." He waves goodbye to Ike and disappears down the log pathway, out of our lives forever.

Amanda, Red, Fran, and Myra come out from the shadows and sit around the fire with the guys. Paul comes down from the balcony. We circle the fire and sit on the logs, while Dara make a beat with two sticks and chants in Spanish. Our souls rejoin to form our chain, forged in firelight by the San Pedro cactus reign. Everything sings in unison once more.

Week Nine | Return to Route

Earth has shown me her soul and it is beautiful.
She knows who rules the land and how to connect to the
cosmic ribbon. We've seen the gate to heaven and crossed
the threshold. Time stands still in these eternal lands,
where hours stretch into days and then to weeks, but I
must connect to my path and follow my spirit. It is time to
go further south.

I sit in Terminal Terrestre in Loja, Ecuador. I
know this bus station, I was here five days ago, going the
other way. I reflect on what has transpired and who I met
over the last two months in this country. Loja is my last
stop before the Peruvian border. I smile, awash with
wonder of what still awaits. There are still four more
months until the snow melts and I can go back to Alaska.

Myra, Fran, and Paul are working their way to a
full moon party on the beach in Columbia. I could go with
them. After the party, I can go to Venezuela, south
through Angel Falls, through the rainforest, and then back
up the Andes into Peru. That sounds like a hassle. Let's
not do that.

Ike told me about a route he once took. From Loja,
cross the Peruvian border to the east, then jeep along a
very painful road at Yurimaguas. The last leg is an eight-
day boat to Iquitos in the Peruvian Amazon. This is
shorter and safer than going through Venezuela.

Most visitors take a prop plane to Yurimaguas, but
I can't afford that. I have more time than money. Once in
Iquitos, it's only a few more days to get to Leticia, the 3-
way border between Columbia, Peru, and Brazil. Then I

can follow the Amazon River down to Manaus, Brazil. I can get back to Peru by taking a jeep through Bolivia. No, wait, stop it. I can't be bothered with this either.

Fran, the freckled fire-light girl from either London or Sydney - she wants to see India next year. Maybe I'll meet her there. She also wants me to visit her in Australia. I will do both, but that's later.

Myra, my dear tall Dutch blonde, she wants me to come to Amsterdam. I will graciously accept this invite also and map a future across more continents with both these women, but not yet. We are now headed in opposite directions in South America. Our times together on this continent have ended.

Instead, I map an easier route. I cross the border into Peru in a luxury bus along the silky smooth Pan-American Highway. This isn't the muddy rainforest I just left a month ago. This isn't hours of delays because El Niño weather is creating mudslides and blocked roads. This is the right path, I'm going straight south for five hours, crossing the border at Macará. I am resigned to my fate. I am fearless, I am content, and I am alone - but none of that ever seems to last long.

Week Ten | *Pais Nuevo*

As I cross the border and get my stamp, but my visa for Peru is only for 60 days! My plane home to Seattle leaves from Lima in 120 days. I'll need to extend it by crossing a border and coming back into Peru, and maybe do that twice. Maybe I will go live in Bolivia for a few months. The calendar is ticking, but I just got to Peru!

It's been six hours since I left Loja, through a combination of a bus to the border, a two-hour cab for two dollars, a walk across town to catch another hour-long bus to Piura, Peru, where I now finally sit.

The girls on the Gringo Trail are mostly exotic Europeans. They are smart and always travel in pairs. Two such women are in the lobby as I check into my hostel.

"Hi! How are you two doing?" I am compelled to ask these questions. They seem welcome.

"Yeah good! I'm Katrine and this is Stina." Stina is a tall willowy blonde with legs like trees. She is quiet yet assertive, frail but determined. She's slightly shorter than me, but her long, straight hair seems to stretch her form.

Katrine is the outspoken one. She is the brunette to complement the blonde. She's not my type, but she holds the deeper conversations. They are both savvy travelettes and we quickly bond in this foreign land.

"I'm headed to Chiclayo in the morning."

"So we are too!" Say the Danes. The decisions are easy when the paths are this obvious. The people we meet fortify our filters and establish our psyches, but like Jimena, Monika, Myra, and Fran, I fear the time when comfort evaporates, and the faces rotate.

"What's next?" Katrine asks, wide-eyed, anxious and ready to try anything. They invite me into their graces to maintain safety in numbers. We really should be careful. The Shining Path rebels are still very active in these hills - at least that's what the US Consulate says.

"We can do whatever we want! We can stay in the mountains, we can go to the beach. We can head to the jungle. There's a place called Chachapoyas where the cloud people live. The guy who changed my money said it rains a lot, but the beautiful jungle women there like to dance around naked." That's a strong endorsement for my endorphins, but I don't think this entices the ladies. It only serves to destroy my gentlemanly image.

"I must tell you though," I continue. "The guard at the bank said it is a communist section, but not officially. Some Japanese tourists there were killed there by the Peruvian military." They look at each other and then at me.

"No!" They are both resolute and easily convince me likewise. Instead, for days, Stina, Katrine, and I saunter around the north of Peru by bus, staying off the trails where the guerrillas want to kidnap tourists.

Northern Peru is rich with history and ripe with ruin. It is lush with early civility but has lost many of its cultures to time. Our days are spent exploring the ancient sites scattered across the tops of the Andes.

We hike The Pyramids of Tucumé. The local shamans believe they mark the location of purgatory, which is befitting at this point in this journey. I just left the threshold of heaven and now venture back into the realm of reality. I do not fear the passage between heaven and earth, my immortality has been fortified. I fear no purgatory.

We stop at The Tomb of Sipan. It's been sealed for 1,700 years and was only discovered a decade ago. It's fresh, as far as tombs are concerned. El Señor de Sipan was not a very nice guy. His servants were all buried in his tomb with him, but he cut off their hands and feet to prevent them from escaping into the afterlife. They can't follow him. They need to stay behind on this mortal land to guide his spirit from this earthly realm to the beyond.

We have now settled in Cajabamba, in the highlands. The Incan King Atahualpa made his home here once, amongst the Incan hot springs and the incredible views. Many archeologists live here now, searching for the fabled City of El Dorado made entirely of gold. The three of us hold no illusions that we will find El Dorado. Yet, we still make snarky conversations about untold wealth to keep us occupied on the bus rides through the countryside and around the mountains.

Week Twelve | Enfermado
Cajabamba, Peru, altitude 8,700 feet.

My rotten sentiments of this city are now a negative side effect of being deathly ill for the last three days. My breath is shallow and my head is throbbing. I'm a constant stream of liquid from both ends and I can't rehydrate. I haven't eaten since we got here. My Valdez baptism proved that I can survive for at least a week without food, but that was easier. I wasn't depleting the reserves that I already have in my body! I'm not worried yet though, it's only been three days.

My head is about to pop even though I've had eight random pills that the girls brought back after hiking. I'm lightheaded and bed ridden. I only rise to use the toilet, which is continual. I can only imagine how my room smells, I've been in here too long to notice. I wish I had some coca leaves, or maybe a hospital, neither of which can be found in Cajabamba.

The human body digests food differently at high altitudes than it does at sea level. The drop of the barometer, the lack of atmospheric pressure - it interrupts the internal organs and the natural flow. It could be from zig-zagging up and down, from mountains to beaches for the last two weeks. Maybe it's an ancient Incan curse, or maybe it's just the beer, but whatever the cause - I am hurting.

Stina and Katrine have been going on short hikes in the day, while I try to get my feet underneath of me. The girls come back with juice, pills, hugs and kisses, but this cannot go on forever. "We've been here too long, we need to change something. You're not getting better," Katrine says lovingly.

"You need doctor," Stina adds. "We also need to get to Lima for our flight." They urge me to join them on a bus down the mountain, but I am too ill to move. I also don't want to shit my pants on a five-hour bus, which I most certainly will if I leave my room for more than ten minutes.

"I'll take the next bus, I'm not packed yet." My excuse is only partly true. I would rather embarrass myself in the company of strangers than in front of these two fine women. Whatever the destination, I know that I must descend - and soon.

"Skål! Bunden i vejret eller resten i håret! Bottoms up, or the rest is in your hair!" We have shared this customary Danish cheer throughout the pubs, the parks, and across the countryside for the last week, but this time it is bitter with double meaning.

"I will miss you two Danishes, my dear donuts."
It's an inside joke. After hugs and kisses, they turn and
walk out of my room forever.

This is not the closing I anticipated, but they don't
need to wait for me here in Cajabamba until I get better. I
am certain I will be fine, I'm still immortal.

I wiggle and wince for the next sixteen hours as I
try to sleep. When I wake, I realize I don't want to die in a
hotel room alone. I must take a chance. I loathe the
thought of expelling liquid on a public bus, but I am not
where I am supposed to be. This is not my path. If I stay
any longer, it may kill more than just my spirit.

I'll descend tomorrow, and if I don't improve, I'll
stop at the first hospital I see, probably in Trujillo, six
hours away if there are no mudslides.

First, I must leave my room. I hug the handrail
and slowly go down the rickety staircase at my hostel.

"I don't see you, I thought you leave!" The hostel
owner is surprised. I haven't been downstairs since I
checked-in with the girls four days ago.

"I've been sick, but I need to leave now. I haven't
eaten for a while." I'm not in the mood for a conversation,
I just need to buy a bus ticket to Trujillo.

"I have la cura, I make you better. Exit here, go left
200 meters, cross the street and tell Taki that I send you.
Confiame." He has great confidence as he says this. He
knows something and wants to share his secret.

I stop at the corner shop and meet Taki. She sits
me down and serves me chicken soup. The soup contains
the head and feet of the chicken, which bubble to the

surface when stirring. Gross. I am not interested in trying to figure out how to eat a chicken head or its feet, these parts promptly exit my dish. I raise the bowl to my lips, expecting my mouth or stomach to reject it, as it has with all food since I first arrived in Cajabamba.

The broth becomes a pure elixir. I feel a resurgence of strength enter my body. The gut-wrenching heaves subside, and my sphincter finally relaxes. But not too much. I am optimistic yet still wary about the bus I am about to board.

The next five hours pass in fleeting fear that my bowels will betray me again. I hold a plastic bag in my hand as I lean next to a window. I feel my body forgiving me, but I am still pale and queasy.

The knots in my stomach release their grip as the barometric pressure returns with each passing mile. We arrive on the coast. The bus stops at a restaurant and I am the first to exit. The last six hours have been spent in fear that I would never get here, but the moment has arrived. I am back at sea-level and perfectly healed. There is no more pain in my head and I can breathe again.

I order a vodka with lychee while I wait for my well-deserved meal. I am fragile yet tranquil, at peace on the beach, descended from the mountain, my soul at ease.

Sama Say Atacama

18

Week Fourteen | February

Two weeks pass in blistering, midsummer's heat and an endless cycle of buses and hostels. The area flourishes with sites like The City of the Dead, The Sarcophagi of Karajia, and The Stone Forest. I soak the Incan culture into my pores. I am living in a nostalgic present, taking mental snapshots and archiving them for later retrieval, for a time when I may find myself with less blissful sentiments.

I stumble upon Chavin de Huantar. This is the birthplace of the Incan culture and belief systems, the seed that planted it all. The Chavin people influenced the continent for centuries, but the site was deserted three thousand years ago, before even Christ walked out of Bethlehem. Even after their decline, their influence stretched for millennia.

Chavin sits on a 10,000-foot-high plateau. The sparse ground vegetation is spotted only by a few scrubby trees. Although there is no quarry here, the fortress walls are built from massive stones. These stones are not found anywhere else in Peru and we're on top of a peak.

Large carved heads chiseled from granite protrude from the walls to guard the priests, the people, and the spirits that once lived within. These stone heads are cut in the forms of spirit animals, human hybrids, and scary monsters, all daring us to misbehave.

The Chavin constructed an elaborate tunnel system. The steps behind the altar of human sacrifice leads the way down into a winding labyrinth. Rectangular stones, mortared with mud, line the ground, the walls, and the ceiling. The expansive tunnels are dark and damp, but wide enough for an elephant, not that they have those here in Peru.

Chavin is an agricultural center for the region, but that's just a cover. There is also an abundance of both hallucinogenic mushrooms and the mighty San Pedro cactus, which are the roots of the Incan and Mayan faiths.

Wild llamas graze on the other side of the complex. We do not phase them, they have seen wilder people. A thousand Andeans used to come here, transposed by San Pedro, burning sage and chanting incantations. Sounds like a righteous party, one that started a religion and a culture. What lives they lived.

Week Fifteen | Second Base

Peru is the crossroads for travelers coming up from Chile, down from Ecuador, or from Brazil in the east. I've seen Peru's roots, the cradle of the culture and their eons of existence, but I want to see what the country has become since these ancient times. I want to see Lima, the capital of modern Peru.

My stomach and I are done with the mountains for a while. It's only an eight-hour bus if I take the Pan-American Highway straight to Lima. I know what I need to do, the path is clear again.

I've been in the country for nearly a month and I'm only halfway to the capital. Staring out of the chicken bus window, crammed with locals and baskets, I wave to the kids in the street. They think I'm a movie star. These moments allow me to reflect and reset.

I discretely reassess my finances and scribble the figures in my journal. I need to prolong the honeymoon, plan the remaining route, and accurately determine my level of luxury.

It is easy to stretch cash and time when hotels are $7, meals are $2, and transportation pays for itself in time spent thinking. I still have $1,200 to get me through the next nine weeks. If I go to Bolivia it's even cheaper, there is enough time and money to keep this comfortable. I've been down here for a while and I'm still perfectly on track.

I take a taxi from the bus station to the Catacomb Church. "We're here, the catacombs are just over there," my driver says. I'm staying at Hostel España, across the street from the convent. Lima is my new home, and Hostel

España is my new base. The view from my room on the roof looks out directly at the towering cathedral. I have stopped. I am here.

"Cuanto es?" I pay my fare, expel my pack from his trunk, and watch him drive away. There is a steady trickle of foot traffic around the plaza, leading to the cathedral tower. Locals and foreigners alike come here to make this pilgrimage to the macabre.

Entering the hostel, the colonial architecture provides a broad courtyard serving as the centerpiece for the building's interior. A balcony serves as the overwatch to the social area. It circles the second floor and stretches the perimeter looking down from all directions. In one corner of the balcony, there's a stairway lined with potted ferns that leads to the rooftop. My room is up here, next to the garden terrace.

I drop my pack and make my personal pilgrimage to the catacombs across the street. The church contains the remains of 25,000 deceased. On the first floor, the nuns tend to the work of their convent. They hold service and greet visitors, but downstairs, a mysterious pit of skulls and bones lie petrified in an eternal graveyard.

I'm not in the mood, I vow to come back later.

At my hostel, a European couple sits at one of the tables, drinking coffee and chatting. Another group of four sit by the stone fireplace and drink Cusqueña beer. They check me out as I check myself in. I find an empty table, determine which crowd would accept me, and order a beer. The coffee-drinkers turn away and the table of four calls me over.

"I'm Nelly, and this is Alex, Roni, and Jacob. We're from Israel." We wave and nod. "We've just arrived and will be here for a week, do you have any suggestions?"

"I have seen most of the north, but it took me four weeks to go a thousand kilometers! The last place I slept is an eight-hour bus ride away. I don't think I'm the best person to address such an expedient itinerary." I pause for effect. "...but I do have some ideas!"

I continue, "I'll probably go to Southern Peru to see the Nazca Lines, then to Cuzco to see Machu Pichu. Then maybe bus over to Bolivia to see the Salt Flats."

Their excited eyes brim with eagerness. "We're going to Cusco tomorrow! I don't think we'll go to Bolivia though." They pause for their own effect and shoot each other inquisitive glances. "You should come with us!"

"Apparently, I was unclear about my pace. I'm slow. I just got into Lima an hour ago, and I'm not ready to hit the road again yet." I speak the truth.

Travel partners come and go, and friends can be found anywhere. There is no reason to latch onto this group immediately. "I have a few more months to explore, and I want to get to know Lima first." They understand. We quip about the Chavin, Sipan, and the misplaced Pyramids. We talk about northern Peru, the ruins, and the Quechua culture.

"You can see most of these wonders in their condensed form simply by going to Cusco! Since you're going anyway, you might just want to spend the whole week in this epicenter." This would be appropriate to their

217

schedules. They are on their right path and I am on mine. We bid adieu and all retire to our separate rooms.

Morning breaks and I hear murmurs in the street below. A ray of light partners with the warm dusty air to penetrate the cracks in my wooden shutters. I look at my travel clock, it says 2:17 pm. I should wake up and go eat.

At the corner café, two local Limeño guys make themselves comfortable before I even realize they are approaching. "Where you from, what you do, I'm Jason!" He pauses and points to the other guy, "and this is Diego."

The conversation quickly digresses, revealing their true intents. "I have girls and I have liquor. You like both, yeah?" Diego is shady, but Jason just seems naïve to this, like he wants a partner to join in whatever this is.

"Sure, let's see where this goes!" I say to Jason. He smiles while Diego shuffles excitedly in his seat. "Can I finish eating?" I say in English, to establish my dominance. They sit with me until I finish my lunch, they seem harmless. Then we all go back to Jason's house.

Diego makes a phone call and invites three girls to his house. I quickly learn that Diego is a Trafficante, or said less elegantly: a pimp, or maybe even a human trafficker, I don't know which, but it's nefarious.

He wants to sell the girls to me by the hour. I get the impression that these girls don't want to be rented out and can't think beyond tonight. This is not where we are supposed to be. When did I meet Jason, an hour ago? It doesn't matter, we're going to the discoteque.

No night is sane. The owner of the discothèque invites Jason and me backstage to smoke pasta. No, not that kind of pasta. Remember the coca leaves in Otovalo, chewed with the enzyme stone to combat altitude sickness? Those leaves are routed to Peru for processing into what resembles toothpaste, which is sent north again to Columbia where it becomes a powder.

We sit in mellow moods, smoke pasta, and chat with the band. We are immediately welcomed since we are foreign, but there is distaste from the locals that are eyeing us. They must prove their worth, unlike us who have just been propped up with the band.

I wake up in my room on the hostel rooftop. I'm not sure how I got here. I look around. My bed is empty, aside from me. I breathe a sigh of relief, quickly followed by a gasp of despair.

There isn't much entertainment in my room, this is just where I sleep. I get dressed, have my coffee in the commons, and head to the corner cantina for breakfast as I have done every morning for the last week. I walk around town. Sometimes I have a destination, but like today, I usually prefer to wander and see what finds me.

A girl abruptly approaches me from the crowd of pedestrians. She's slender and dirty, with natty hair. Her clothes are rags, but mine are too. I can't judge. She puts her hand on my arm and looks me in the eye. She speaks to me for minutes, barely stopping to breathe. She speaks fast but her words are empty. In the last five minutes, all I've learned is that her name is Priscilla.

I try to make my escape. She grabs my hand in hers and follows me down the sidewalk as if we're traveling Peru together! She is local. She is very poor, a little desperate, and completely crazy. She has a tenacity that makes me mildly curious, but not overtly. I like her - but this won't blossom beyond its present novelty.

I've tried my most resolute, but I cannot shake her. She even jumps in my cab with me as I leave the plaza! I guess we're going to the museum *together*. She doesn't want to come inside with me, which is perfect, I don't want to lead her on by paying her entrance fee.

I've been in the museum for ninety minutes, and she's still sitting outside. I have a stalker. I exit the museum hug the fence line, and slide right past Priscilla. I hop into the nearest cab and return to my hostel. I leave her stranded on the stairs of the museum. She knows these streets, she'll figure it out.

I wake up for my afternoon breakfast. Heavy foot traffic funnels into the corner bar, creating small dust clouds that hover above the street. It seems there are new faces at Hostel España. One new face named Jerry stops to chat with me.

Jerry is energetic, but not yet road worn. He just got into the country five days ago. He's a wholesome American boy, with well-prepared hair, clean clothes, and sparkly teeth. His face gleams with innocence. We are the same age, but he hasn't been in the military or addicted to drugs. He is pure and I can smell it. We share a meal and a conversation, but very soon we may share much more.

"I met this girl and I think I love her!" The conversation with Jerry turns nauseating, and my attention drifts away, choosing to listen to my own thoughts instead. I am alerted back to the present again when he says, "Let's go get the girls and go to the pub!" Oh yeah, that's what Jerry was trying to say before all that gooey babble.

Jerry met Sama at Machu Pichu just a few days ago, but that's a lifetime when you're traveling. Sama is traveling with her homegirl Val from Argentina, which makes them mostly local here in Peru. They are out to explore their own continent. Jerry and the girls have shared experiences from Machu Pichu over the last few days and have had opportunities to bond. I am new.

We spend the evening on the patio under an umbrella with a cool city breeze, laughing and drinking. We talk about our own unique worlds, and how those worlds have collided, bringing us together at the same place, here at this disco in Lima.

It takes only minutes to learn that Jerry doesn't speak any Spanish at all! I spend most of the evening translating between him and Sama, which is odd considering his professed love for her. I grow weary of repeating everything in English and my attention drifts far, far away from Jerry and much closer to Sama.

Sama's jubilant and playful character mesmerizes me. She is experienced, she likes to live life and take risks. She has the physique of a runner and the face of a model, accented by her golden-brown hair. Her Argentinian accent sounds like a songbird serenading the moon.

Week Sixteen

I've been to all the sites in Lima multiple times, usually with different groups of people. I'm the gringo guide, indoctrinating new arrivals into the land. But when I meet Sama, we map an entirely different route around the moon and out to the stars.

Two days pass and Jerry melts into the woodwork. Val has been spending time with some friends she knows here in Lima, while Sama and I walk the markets and visit my favorite five sites. Sama and I have the chemistry that Jerry thinks they have.

We are on our way to the catacombs, when a homeless girl jumps wildly in front of us, stopping us cold in our tracks. I haven't seen my stalker Priscilla for a week, and she is enraged! After our museum trip, she continued the fantasy that we are courting, and she's mad because I haven't been home to see her in a week! Further, I am now cheating on her with Sama, walking hand-in-hand down the paseo.

"Where you been, WHY YOU LEAVE??" Priscilla shouts in my face, turning heads in the street. "We have a thing and you disappear!"

I plead with Sama that I've never seen this girl before in my life – until Priscilla calls me by name. Sama looks at me, and for a fleeting moment, I see jealousy, mistrust, and anger. She pauses, releases my arm, and walks away. I follow Sama like a kicked puppy. It takes some explaining, but she eventually comes to understand how I shared a taxi with and a museum visit with this schizophrenic local, and why she is now in love with me.

"It's my irresistible magnetism," I tell Sama. She chortles, looks at me sideways, and drops the whole thing. We grasp hands and walk as quickly as we can to escape Priscilla and her madness.

We meet up with Val back at the hostel, and we begin to hatch our plan. "Where are we going next? You want to go to Chile with us? And then we can all go to Buenos Aires!" Sama and Val ask me together in their sing-songy accents.

It takes only a mild shoulder nudge from Sama for my clock and compass to start spinning erratically. This is the moment, the cornerstone, the intersection to make a decision that shapes a person and detours the route.

"You can stay at my house in my room, my family will be cool with that! I'll save some cash, and then we can go to Alaska together." I wonder if this is the right time to tell Sama that I like to move slowly. I'm not in a rush.

"You're going where, you want to what?!" I usually have good impulse reflexes, but I don't think the girls have thought this through. It would take two months for Sama to save for a ticket to get all the way back to Alaska. I can get a job for her in Valdez easy enough though.

"This might work! One significant problem though, I have $800 and eight weeks before my plane leaves." It might be possible to survive in Bolivia, or maybe Peru, but Argentina is different, it is modern.

This will be a challenge. Staying at Sama's house - in her bed - might make up the difference. Of course, none of this is of importance. Our fates are fortified. "Si, como no!" Why not, I say to the girls.

The Escape

19

I've made it overland from my arrival city of Quito to my departure port of Lima. I've completed my planned route. For the last ten days, I have been tethered to Lima, not sure where to go, but if I venture as far as Argentina, my tether may snap.

The girls reject the plan to go through Bolivia and Paraguay to get to Argentina. It would be a cheaper route with more jungle, and it would give me time to think about this, but the girls want to hug the coastline south.

Bolivia must wait. Machu Pichu must wait. I'm going to Chile with Sama and Val! I have two months, but they only have a few weeks before they need to return to their homes in Buenos Aires. I will follow their plans.

I've been drifting on my own breeze for a while, it is a welcome thrill to be swept up in their tornados. The bright shining beacon is fading. My destination is replaced by the brilliance of Sama and the prospect of a future together. First, maybe we should get to know one another. Nah, we can do that in Chile.

Our new destination is four thousand kilometers away, further down the Andes, turn east across the driest desert on Earth, and eventually arrive in Argentina on the opposite side of South America. Two weeks seems too fast.

We leave tomorrow, but the problem is, they paid for a flight out of Lima to the Chilean border town of Tacna. I'm not exactly a jet-setter and this isn't in my budget. Eh, what's the worst that could happen?

After landing, we take a cab ride to the border crossing. We get out next to a modest building flanked by two flags: one Peruvian and one Chilean.

Chile is just on the other side of this building. We step inside. We're the only people here, so we each get our own dedicated customs officials and our own booths. Yay.

The officials escort us into a small area the size of dressing rooms. This is the gateway to a new country. Chile lay's just beyond. I enter, and they close the curtain behind me.

"Lay your bag upon the table," they instruct with impressive English. I still have some leftover pasta in my backpack from that crazy night with Diego El Traficante. The border agents must sense this. They are playful, but they are also threatening.

"Maybe we take everything out of your backpack?"

The pasta is in my bathroom bag, which seemed like a good place since it looks like toothpaste. It's unlikely that these border guards would find it even if they decide to dig deeper, but still, I don't need their hands fondling my things. That could possibly lead to a Chilean prison and other people fondling my things. I doubt the quantity I have would land such a penance, but I don't want to press my luck.

"How much money do you have?" says one guard.

"I changed everything before I came to this border! I'm waiting to find a bank in Chile to cash some traveler's checks for pesos. I gave my Peruvian soles to the taxi driver!" It's true, I have the equivalent of about $2 in random change. I figure they don't want me to sign over my traveler's checks unless they want a paper trail leading to their bribe. I have no use for the coins in my pocket and I hand them to the officer. They are visibly discouraged and annoyed. They want a big American payday, but instead, they got me.

While I've been chatting with the guards for the last twenty minutes, deflecting the gentlest of interrogations, another bus arrives. The girls went straight through to Chile and have been waiting for me on the other side. I peek through the curtain from my booth and see some faces that were on the airplane from Lima.

The officials pull back the curtain and let me pass into Chile, so I can meet up with Sama and Val. The girls want to know what took me so long, but I spare them any details of the customs officials soliciting me for bribes, or that technically I still have drugs in my backpack.

Walking towards the taxis, the first image we see are two rows of about twenty severed goat heads lining each side of the walkway. Their eyes are rolled back in their heads and their tongues are hanging out, licking the dirt like a giant salt block. The stump of their necks has left little red puddles, demonstrating their freshness. We walk between these rows like a sinister wedding to find our waiting taxi.

Seeing these severed goat heads, I wonder if the universe is trying to tell me something. It's difficult to know, we haven't spoken since Vilcabamba. Parading a row of slaughtered goat heads at a primary land crossing seems to be a profane way to greet visitors. Maybe it's a sign or maybe that's just customary in Chile.

Two older ladies from the plane each grab a goat head by the horns and walk over to the man sitting on the wooden stool. They hand him some wrinkled cash. These bloody goat heads must serve some purpose other than just to scare tourists. The ladies each put their goat head on the back of their mopeds and scurry away, presumably back to their homes here in northern Chile.

A three-hour bus takes us to Arica, a dry little city surrounded by deserts and mirages. Charles Darwin once described Arica as "a town very much in want of everyday necessities, such as water and firewood." I don't need firewood, but I concur, this place is lacking. Charles and I have different needs, but Arica meets none of them. We find a bar that serves half-meter tall mojitos and proceed to waste two days here.

Over the next week, we take buses to the beach towns of Iquique, Mejillones, and Antofagasta. We hop down the coastline looking for greenery, but we find only shrubs. The ocean is our friend, but there seems to be no escape from the otherwise dull dryness of northern Chile and her barren earth.

After wandering aimlessly, we turn inland, arriving at the doorstep of the Atacama Desert. The town is dotted with crumbling man-made structures, struggling to bestow refuge to road-weary travelers. That's us.

Six conical volcanoes dot the skyline, encircling the high plateau. The surrounding low lands have been baked clean of foliage, exposing the cracked earth and the raw derma underneath.

Week Seventeen | Valentine's Day

The tires churn up the gritty sand as our bus pulls away from San Pedro de Atacama (a city that has nothing to do with the cactus. Saint Peter has many influences).

The Atacama Desert is the driest in the world. It is geographically positioned between two opposing cloud voids, a two-sided rain shadow, forever exiling the water cycle. All moisture has long since evaporated, leaving behind silvery salt lakes.

No new rain falls, some parts haven't seen rain for 400 years. Life is dead out here. The more tropical parts might see an inch annually. Mother Nature has forsaken it since the last ice age. This cracked Earth has an insatiable thirst and is in dire need of a drink, much like us. We walk to the only café in the village.

Today is Valentine's Day and I'm with my sweetheart. Thankfully, she doesn't expect flowers - they would have to be imported. I fashion a rose from a napkin I have in my pocket, a trick I learned a few months ago in a Quito bar with Jimi. I hand my rose napkin to Sama. "Happy Valentine's Day!" Sama chortles.

Sama needs to call her madre. She still hasn't told her that I am coming to live with them - or that Sama is moving to Alaska with me!

"She said ok." Sama relays her mamma's response. Sama's tone is tense, she is shielding me from what her mother really said. I can guess.

This is a quiet town. We are the only ones on the street, but we see two bicycles next to a lamp post a block away. Passing a patch of golden grass on the sidewalk, we enter the café. A man and woman are talking to the owner. "Wow, people!" I say loud enough for them to hear.

"Yeah, we're here," the girl grumbles. "We had an expedition today but it's too bloody hot. We'll have to wait until nightfall. I'm a geologist and Rich here is a photographer." I see a few bags of equipment and what looks like a camera case next to the wall.

"This heat will change the composition of our exhibit, but I think we can make it work," Rich says. "We can try again tomorrow too, since the bus doesn't leave until Thursday."

"La clima no es tipico," the hostel owner says. He claims that this 115°F climate is unusual. "It's usually quite pleasant here." I wonder if a volcano is about to blow. That would be neat.

"All of the shop owners have gone to the coast where it's cooler. It's just me and the hostel that are open now." They are all escaping to where we just left, the coast. We will not be hiking here, we will not be partying here, there will be no joy. I don't like Chile and this desert heat makes it even more miserable.

"Wait! Rich, what do you mean *Thursday*?! That's two days away!" Rich confirms with a nod and a sly smirk, like he's ashamed to be enjoying himself in this wasteland.

"Yes, two more days."

Val is visibly agitated, looking at the floor and shifting from side to side. The girls and I all look at each other, whisper, and agree that there is nothing here for us. We can't wait until Thursday, we don't even want to wait until tomorrow. We are ready to go now! *And so we shall.*

Val and I lament our situation, we both prefer green forests, while Sama is suspiciously quiet, since this Atacama route was her idea. I'm still considering going north to Bolivia by myself and ditching these fine girls. We've only known each other for a week in Peru and a week across northern Chile. The road north to Bolivia is only a few hours behind us in Calama, and the bus going that way leaves tomorrow, not Thursday.

"You can try hitchhiking out of here, trucks come sometimes," says the grumbly girl, while Rich nods again, still sly. Maybe that's just his face.

"There's nothing here and we won't wait two days for the bus," Val snarls. "Maybe someone will take us." We don't care about the mode of transport, or even where it goes, just that it comes soon and takes us elsewhere.

I look at the girls and attempt to strike a compromise. "I hitchhike a lot in Alaska, we can try it here! If we don't get picked up, we'll go to Bolivia tomorrow." I have no confidence that we'll find a ride.

"Ok, we'll do that," Val quickly agrees, speaking for Sama who remains quiet. We've all just landed on Mars and our spaceship left about twenty minutes ago. Maybe if we run we can still catch it.

We stock up on water, exit the shop, and walk to the edge of town. The customs station to exit Chile is just a bus stop, with one bench, walled in on three sides by plywood. This is the last checkpoint before crossing the border from Chile into Argentina, but there is no one here. There is no one to say goodbye.

Over the next five hours, two cars pass, but neither stops for us. We've been sitting here in the dry, blistering heat, watching the options disappear. The scarcity of vehicles makes it even more painful when they don't stop. They don't care that we are here. This is the exact opposite of how this works in Alaska.

We must adjust our approach. There is a small berm on the side of the road, just deep enough for me to hide behind. It might be easier if I let these two beautiful girls hitchhike alone, don't mind me, I'll just be hiding in the bushes ready to pounce if anyone stops for us.

I know this power of feminine allure all too well. I have been detoured by pairs of ladies many times over the last few months. Sam and Val use their appeal and show some leg to the next car. Unless it's an old lady that drives by, this should get us a ride the hell out of this oven.

231

Another hour passes before our next great hope arrives in the form of a semi-truck coming over the horizon. The ladies wave seductively. The truck approaches and stops. It works!

There are two men inside that could be brothers. Each has dark, stubbly facial hair. I make a mental note, as I learned when I trained to be a marine. Two average white males, jeans and T-shirts, 25-35 years of age, 170 pounds, brown hair, no visible scars or markings. Yeah, they could be anyone.

Peeking over the dirt, I see the passenger offer his hand to help Sama into the cab. If at this moment, my lovely traveling partners decide to leave without me, or if these truckers are into kidnapping and murder, their end could be near. If that door closes, it is entirely possible that Sama and Val will never be seen alive again - or me for that matter. I would flail behind choking on the dust until the truck disappears as quickly as it came.

The girls are hesitant to enter, but Val looks my way, making me feel the need to rush to their aid that's my cue, I must announce my presence and my intentions. Bouncing out of the bushes, I shout a quirky "Hola! Gracias hombres!" I climb the steps, wiggle past the passenger, and see a raised mattress behind the two front seats. The two men sleep here on long trips, and perhaps they had other intentions with the girls on this particular long ride, but this is now our space. It will be our front row seats to the miles of dirt that are to follow.

"Thanks for the ride!" I proclaim in my Ecuadorian accent, tinged with Americana and naiveté.

Sama and Val sit on either side of me while the two men are now visibly annoyed. For hours, I protect the girls from wandering hands, mal intents, and lustful advances. As I drift to sleep, Sama pinches my thigh, jolting me back to the disturbing conversations. She appreciates my presence and my illusion of protection. The checkpoint is still three hours east through this isolated land.

Time stretches behind as the road stretches ahead. Machu Pichu and Bolivia are distant mirages in the rear-view mirror. I wonder if these horny truckers will murder me and leave me for dead in the desert. Will I die upon a mound, beaten by the sun and whipped by the sand?

Like my psyche as a soldier balanced against the pressures of freedom, or the depression of addiction weighed against the bliss of the beaches, these polar extremes define me. They give me cause to feel alive! Unfortunately, everything is dead out here.

The Atacama Desert is barren, and the Alaskan wilderness is refreshing. These contrasts are defined by the other's seasons and provide the yin yang to complement the other. The extremes balance the inside with the out, the mind with the body, defining the route.

In this part of Chile, there are no trees, no streams, and no ducks. This Atacama earth is thirsty. Life feels deserted in this land without water. The hard dirt road takes us closer towards the Atlantic Ocean, away from the Pacific countries like Ecuador, Peru, and now Chile. We roar towards the coast, but first we must get across these damn mountains and deserts!

Our cargo truck creates tiny dust tornadoes behind us, but inside the cab, other things are stirring. The innuendos are difficult to decipher in Chilean jargon, but the wandering hands of our hosts are unmistakable. They want to share the girls. I playfully slap their hands away, but this joke is getting old. The girls each have their hand on my thigh, claws out, concerned that this may escalate.

The two men wish I never jumped out from behind that bush and startled them with "Gracias hombres!" They would much rather I jump out of this truck now and roll down a hill, leaving them to their advances unhindered.

After an eternity of battling for chastity, another building comes into view. This is a checkpoint, but unlike the bus stand in San Pedro, this one is an actual building and a man is standing outside. It's a humble building, serving as a hybrid between a park ranger's office, the Chilean Embassy, and a deserted outpost.

Val exits and is greeted by the armed border guard. "Miss, welcome. Are you all passing into Argentina?"

"Sir, no. Not yet. We need a place to stay tonight."

The truckers come closer to listen. Val continues, "...but they can't stay here! Please ask them to keep driving," Sama says, glaring at the truckers, while explaining the situation to the guard.

The guard doesn't hesitate. He ushers us to stand near the building while he talks to them. They exchange some very angry words. I don't fully understand, but their body language acutely conveys their disgust. The guard casually puts his hand at his hip, perched atop his pistol.

The two men climb into their truck, roar the engine, and disappear down the road.

"This way, please." The guard escorts us inside and treats us right. He shows us to our cots where we will lay our weary heads tonight. He walks away to tend his desk and leaves us to get settled.

"We're staying here tonight!" Val screams.

"...and those guys are gone!" Sama adds.

The girls are excited, but to me this feels a lot like yesterday: stuck in San Pedro de Atacama without a bus for two days. We don't care what comes next, we just want to shower and wash the Chilean sand from our ears and be safe from the snakes of the desert.

The outpost is a sanctuary where weary travelers rest and recover. It is quiet and dark here, miles from anywhere, but this is the most luxury we've had in days. Our sleeping quarters are like barracks, but I don't think I'll hear reverie at 5 am. Even the cold, concrete floor reminds me of boot camp.

A short wall separates the cots from a dimly lit shower room, akin to what you might see in a prison or a high-school gym. In the Marines, we called them rain-trees. I hated them then, but I don't mind them now, in the dusty heat, sharing the scene with Sama and Val.

The three of us are the only ones here, aside from the guard out front protecting us. It feels like everyone escaped the apocalypse, but we missed the notification.

First Val and Sama shower together, washing each other clean from the advances of dirty men. I cautiously join them and we all shower together as if the world is about to end. This is my redemption, my reward for serving, a difficult memory washed anew.

Morning breaks. We step outside and confirm that we are still in the desert. Dammit. We need to travel for five more hours before the land will start turning green again. The bus is still a full day behind us, and this outpost is no place to spend the day. We need to find our way out again. We need to hitch, but most cars should stop here.

I mumble "Bolivia" under my breath begrudgingly while kicking at the dirt. We are here now, and we don't want to be stuck in the heat. The Atacama is for scientists and geologists, not the three of us. After a few more cups of yerba de maté, our host returns from the back room with our passports - complete with Chilean exit stamps. We pack our bags and head out the door, like weeds tumbling down a dusty road, wanting for more.

For two hours, there are no cars, but then a little red truck stops. An older man with a cowboy hat and wrinkly skin rolls down the window. He puts his elbow out. "What are you doing out here?" he asks in a drawled Spanish dialect I've never heard before.

"Trying to get out of here!" I respond in a Quechua accent, thinking it would help me blend in. He squints his eyes, trying to understand what I am.

"Ya vamos," he says. Val climbs hastily into the front, while Sama and I lay out my sleeping bag in the back. The gateway to Argentina, Paso de Jama, lies 250 km and four hours ahead of us, where we can retrieve our entry stamps to Argentina and return to civilization.

We are officially without a country. What is this place in between? It is unworthy of being claimed by any nation and this road is a mere pass through from here to there. It mirrors the mantra of my existence; I am not where I am, but have not yet arrived to where I will be. I am in between.

Week Seventeen | *February 15*

Northern Chile is stripped of color, drowned in brown with a sunburnt and cracked landscape. As we descend the desert plateau, scattered trees come into view, a checkpoint, then more trees, then we see grass, and even a few buildings. There are concrete streets and lawns with sprinklers. Just as the sun is setting, we arrive in Salta, the largest city in northern Argentina. We made it.

I have crossed another threshold, snapped my tether, committing Peru, Ecuador, and Chile to memory. Machu Pichu and Bolivia are now unfulfilled prospects of a dreamer, melted away in the blaze of the desert sands.

The wrinkled man in his red truck delivers us to the city park in the middle of Salta. Amidst soccer fields and tennis courts, wide patches of grass dance under big oak trees. There are no other tents around, but the girls assure me that camping here is perfectly acceptable. I'm just happy for the opportunity to use the tent that I have been carrying around for the last four months.

Hitchhiking has been nearly impossible in South America, but we can camp openly in the middle of a public park. Hitching in Alaska is easy, but there's nowhere to camp in all the vast wilderness. I will never understand this earth or the rules of man.

The flowers are blooming and the scent of pollen hangs in the warm summer air. The civilians have left the park, it is ours for the evening. Val leaves to explore the city while Sama and I stay behind to rock the tent in a steamy exhilaration, joined in an expression of elation to be back in civility. We celebrate.

The long drive has forced us to molt through many mixed emotions, but we now share a sense of security and relief. Sama and I desperately need a shower, so we head to the locker rooms in the middle of the park.

It's almost 8 pm, it's dark, and the air is quiet. There is one lady in the woman's locker room, so we go to the men's locker room instead. It is empty. It is dark and we cannot find the light switch. We prefer it dark anyway.

Everything seems closed for the night, and we don't expect any interruptions. A sliver of moonlight is coming through the windows, we don't need the lights on.

Five shower stalls line each side of the men's locker room, with a row of benches in the middle. Like the outpost, cement walls divide the showers, but without the rain trees. We undress, throw our clothes on the bench, and chose a shower.

After taking turns sharing a bar of soap and the slow stream of warm water for ten minutes, a voice outside surprises and freezes us mid-lather. The voice gets closer and is followed by another, much quieter jabber. A young father and a little boy walk in. The kid is quick and neither of them see us. They stand outside of the building and talk, but their voices soon dissipate. We are alone again. It's just the three of us, Sama, the soap, and me.

The door slams open against the wall! A swarm of young guys enter. They jeer and boast like they just got done with a fútbol game and they are the winning team. They swiftly find and flick-on the light switch that Sama and I had tried so desperately to find before.

Our eyes and our moods try to adjust to the sudden influx of both light and people. Our thoughts turn to escape, but it is only now that we realize our clothes are by the entrance, on the other side of our new shower mates who sit on the center benches.

That isn't a good place for our clothes, we need them before we can escape this situation and return to our tent. I don't think I should ask Sama to prance over there. Oddly, she's oddly the only naked girl in this crowded men's locker room. I also don't want to leave my naked girlfriend in the shower alone, on my first day in this country, with a sweaty and jubilant fútbol team.

This will be a three-part escape. First, I thoroughly lather Sama with bubbles to obscure her hot feminine form. Second, I wait until the guys are in their showers so I can quickly grab our clothes without fear of "where you from" conversations. The third part is to rinse, dry, clothe, and run to our tent as fast as we can!

A few of the men see me, but don't appear concerned that we are here, nor that we are naked. No one looks twice. They are not talking about us and there are no judgmental glances. It feels like either Sama and I are invisible ghosts, or this sort of thing happens frequently in

Salta. On a continent where my appearance has made me very conspicuous, I am relieved to now be unnoticed.

Sama and I look at each other, mystified as to whether the team is just being courteous, or if they are truly oblivious. It doesn't much matter, it only makes this easier. It is time to enact the escape plan.

I meet a few glances as I scan the room awkwardly, my chin tucked into my chest. I grab our clothes and return to Sama within a few seconds. I hold Sama's towel while she rinses. She foregoes her bra and panties for the sake of expediency, pulling her skirt flush with her flesh. I pull on my shorts and put my shirt on backwards.

With my arm around Sama, we run away from the building, through the trees, clutching our towels and laughing in the dark. The plan goes perfectly! Sama punches me in the shoulder since it was my idea to shower together in the men's locker room. This might make up for Bolivia, I haven't decided yet.

Salta is not a destination for us, it is a break in the monotony, a location of surrender, before continuing ahead searching for something better. The bus station in Salta is considerably more active than the last one in San Pedro where our spaceship stranded us. The three of us buy our tickets for the last 1,500 km stretch to Buenos Aires. We will be there in seventeen hours.

We book the luxury bus, kick back, and stare out the window for the day. Sama collapses into my lap. I wrap my hand around Sama's side, between her breasts, cradling her cheek like a little kitten. I stare out the window and into the night as the wheels hum along.

The Wooden Port

20

Month Five | Home Away

Two spontaneous lovebirds in Lima hatched a plan to live with momma bird in Buenos Aires, and then fly across the hemisphere to the top of North America. Birds migrate, that's what we do.

The trees that started to appear outside of Salta are now thinning again. The shacks turn into houses and then into hotels. Quechua natives turn into gauchos and then into businessmen. We arrive in Buenos Aires.

This isn't Machu Pichu, but it provides the solitude for my indulgence into another culture. I have $600, but that means different things in Argentina than it does in Peru or Bolivia. For the cost of a day spent in Buenos Aires, I could sustain four days in Bolivia. If this cash cannot stretch until my flight leaves in six weeks at the end of March, I will need to change my departure date and leave earlier out of Buenos Aires.

As a last resort, if I can't stretch my cash, I can put my culinary experience to work and get a real job in a kitchen. Is this the end of the road? has my trip concluded? My fantasy vacation now feels like real life.

After only a week, I spend most of my money and realize that I took the wrong path to the wrong place. I shouldn't be on the Atlantic coast! I am too far away and I need to get home! I call the airline to reset my ticket to Seattle to depart from Buenos Aires.

"I'm sorry sir, we don't fly to Buenos Aires. The only city we service in South America is Lima, Peru."

I am jolted. I don't know what to say. I was prepared to negotiate the price, but there is no bartering with the fact they don't even fly here! This could prove very disruptive.

My plane leaves from Lima in seven weeks, but I'm on the wrong side of the continent. I open my wallet and examine a few raggedy bills. I have two traveler's checks in reserve, but then the reservoir will be dry. How can I get through these last weeks and get to Lima? I left the gates of heaven and wandered through purgatory, but the walls of both are collapsing inward. The honeymoon is over.

It is not my destiny to become homeless in South America. This is fine in Alaska, there are opportunities and proximities, but not in Argentina. I'm too far from my roots. I am stuck. I can't get home, to my real home, my tether has snapped.

Strike one: I can't stretch my cash long enough. Strike two: I can't change my ticket to fly home from Buenos Aires. I need to activate my third and final contingency: get a job.

Sama's dad sells T-shirts and delivers them using a small wooden ox-cart. He invites me to join his business as his helper, but that doesn't feel like the right life for me. I probably should help anyway, just to pay for room and board, but I'm not that considerate. I keep looking.

Sama helps me make a resume and gives me a nice button-up shirt. I put it on, along with a wide smile, and go to the city's best restaurants. I go door to door, from La Boca to the port, along the boardwalk restaurants, cafés, and any other place that serves food. I need to find a way to survive. Where is my next Unko?

I beat the streets of the dining districts. I'm not legally authorized to work here, and my resume is chock-full of fantastic fictions, but someone will believe me and be willing to pay me under the table. I just need to find that person and their restaurant.

The ritzy places are concentrated down by the water, at El Puerto Madero - The Wooden Port. The bus drops me off a few blocks away from the water, on Avenida 9 de Julio, the world's widest street. I cross twenty-four lanes to get to the other side, passing three pedestrian islands and a huge obelisk jutting into the sky.

I continue to the row of restaurants facing the water. I knock on every door, starting at one end of the pier and migrating to the other. I approach the last establishment on the boardwalk. I enter and walk down the thin hall, which opens to an expansive and ornate dining room. The walls are glass windows that encircle the perimeter, transparently separating us from the outside world. The bar serves as the centerpiece to the dining room, while the patrons look out onto the docks and the world beyond.

The kitchen is just to the right. I walk up to the bar and request to see the manager. We go into his office for about five-minutes and I walk out with a job as a pasta cook! This time, yes, real pasta, not the intermediary stage of cocaine. Pasta like noodles and gnocchi.

On the way out, I take note of the restaurant name and location relative to the pier. I've been walking all day and I will need to find my way back! Restaurante Cholila completes my integration, this will be home, but this life is different than the one I left on the other side of the hemisphere.

I work. I blend. I integrate. The weeks grow into a month, then a few more weeks pass. In Lima, my plane comes and goes, but I am still in Buenos Aires. The reality of an exotic life with Sama do not match the dreams, as we grow distant, and ripples peddle through our paradise.

I go to work at noon and get home around 1:30 am. By then, Sama has already been out for hours and I'm too tired to join the party. When we do go out, it feels artificial. I know this will never be my true home. Sama is the reason I am here, yet she is nowhere near me. I spend more time with her dad watching American talk shows.

Twice a day, I kiss my boss's stubbly face. It's an Argentinian custom to hold each other's shoulders, lean in gently, kiss left - then right, regardless of gender. This is most welcome when visiting Sama's gorgeous friends, but considerably less appealing with Mike.

He is the typical chef, 250 pounds in a dirty apron, with a sparkly five o'clock shadow attempting to conceal his acne skin. We have always been cordial at work, but we don't socialize beyond that.

Mike runs the kitchen but doesn't sign my checks. Unfortunately, no one else does either. I should have been paid twice by now, but I haven't yet received a single Argentinian peso.

I am working here illegally, but I'm also terrible at cooking. They don't feel obligated to pay me. The senior chefs get paid first, then the rest of us get the scraps based on revenue. My cash reserves have dwindled to $7 and I am desperately close to being penniless and homeless in this country. I may have to hitchhike back over the Atacama to get to Peru. I do not want to do that, but I don't know what else to do.

I've been lugging a small tent, a sleeping bag and a rolled-up sleeping mat across this continent for the last five months. My gear was under my bed in Quito when I needed it most, on my trip to the Amazon. I used my sleeping bag once in the wrinkly man's truck getting through the Atacama, and the tent came in handy at the Salta park, but my gear has been mostly dead weight. Maybe it's worth something. I need to sell it for cash.

Back in Alaska, I spent $800 on this camping gear. I could really use that cash now. Funny how these things go. Ironically, if I ever needed to camp in South America, that time is fast approaching. With no money and no home, I could camp in Patagonia and work my way across the mountains, clutching my ticket home.

I call a few camping stores, but they are all closed for the next two days. They take their weekends very seriously. All the stores are closed. I won't be selling anything today. If I don't get paid at work, within a week I will need to beg, borrow or steal on my way to Patagonia. This is going to be an uncomfortable weekend.

Week Twenty-Two | Easter

Since I left Lima with Sama and Val eight weeks ago, my Argentinian immersion has become a punishment to my vacation. I rarely see either of the girls, and I missed my plane to Seattle two weeks ago.

I have drifted from the planned path. The wind was blowing easterly and I hitched a ride on a whim and tailpipe smoke. This detour has led me to work for free, for a boss I hate, with friends I can't understand and an icy girlfriend who stopped holding my hand weeks ago.

Sama has plans with her friends for Easter next weekend, and those plans do not include me. I am supposed to be gone already and I can no longer stay with Sama's family. They don't want me here. I am being exiled. I should be living luxuriously in La Paz, crossing overland until I reach the bright shining beacon of Machu Picchu.

Instead, I am back in the hall of mirrors, desperately searching for the exit. The romance that Sama and I shared has faded, unable to be rekindled. Instead, I will set my beacon ablaze, and return to the wind.

"I quit. I QUIT!" I practice this out loud a few times on my way to Cholila's. I walk through the cook's entrance, greet my friends, say my goodbyes, and explain why I am leaving so abruptly.

For a month, Andrew the accountant has said that I can pick up my check on the following Friday, but every time a Friday comes, I remain poor. They provide a new creative excuse every time I show up. These months of labor have been strictly voluntary, further enabling the depletion of both my financial and emotional reserves. Rock bottom is coming up fast, I know what this feels like.

Andrew now says "you can only get paid on the first Friday of the month," which is fortunately for me – is next Friday! This is suspiciously convenient.

"My wallet is empty. Can I get an advance?"

"Advances are only for those that are currently working. You are not." I did quit, and I would quit again if I could. But now I think I need to be hired again so I can get a cash advance just to make it through the weekend.

I return home, walk back to Sama's room and put on a fresh shirt. I come back out to greet the family.

"What? They didn't pay you?!" says my former future mother-in-law. She is irate. She wants me gone. I want me gone too, but I can't get gone.

Madre barks fervently, "Tell me the restaurant name! I call them and fix this now!"

Sama, her mamma, and I sit around their folding dining table in their small, sanitary, white kitchen. In the center of the table sits the black rotary telephone. She finds the number and calls my boss. For the next ten minutes, mamma yells into the phone.

Sama's eyes are fixated on her mother, and mine are fixed on Sama. These words they are exchanging are new to my vocabulary. I understand the words like lawyer, illegal, foreigner, and advantage, but there is a lot of jargon in rapid fire. Those filler words seem to hold the clues, but possibly it's better to just stay ignorant. I understand enough.

I ask Sama for a translation, but she hushes me. Mom hangs up, pauses, and then walks around the room. Sama grabs my hand and locks eyes. In slow, easy, Spanish words, she proclaims, "It is very serious to work illegal in Argentina."

I am surprised to be on this side of the conversation. In Alaska, restaurants hire workers with false documents who are just trying to survive. Al once yelled "La Migra!" just to see who would run out on their shift trying to escape the immigration police.

I am a broke American in Argentina, tripping over cultural, financial and now legal borders in search of other options. I now know how they feel.

"What happened? What did they say? WHAT?!" I ask Sama. I am ready for her to deliver my fate, which can go only one of two ways. By the looks on their faces, the conversation didn't go very well.

"Am I going to jail?"

"Mom just impersonated a lawyer for you and it worked. They pay you $443 next Friday."

That's all I need to hear. I have burned all the bridges in Buenos Aires. Both Sama and her mamma are furious, like freight trains roaring, billowing steam from their ears. Mamma heads into the other room, but not before grumbling a few more words which have the rough undertone of "... *get the hell out of my house.*"

The week drags slowly by, until my final Friday arrives like Christmas morning. A great payday is upon me. I hop on the 64 bus, cross the great Avenida, pass the obelisk, and skip down to the docks. I go through the front door of the restaurant like I'm a customer, this makes me feel important.

"Is Andrew the Accountant here?"

"Yes, he's behind the bar." I walk over.

Andrew's head is lowered, like a beat dog. This must be how I looked when Sama and mamma were talking to me at the kitchen table.

Mamma's persistence on the phone has sent waves through this entire restaurant. My former waitress friends nod, but they do not talk to me. There are weird glances from the cooks behind the kitchen glass.

"I have your pay, I just need to see your Telegrama de Renuncia," Andrew says from behind the bar, while I perch on a stool and plant my elbows.

The spacious wooden surface acts as a moat between our emotions, our futures, and our discontents. I should not have tried to integrate into this culture, knowing I would not be here indefinitely.

"Sorry, what do I need? A pinche *telegram*?!" I made him repeat himself a few more times.

"You need to mail your letter to us that says you quit. It needs to be marked by the Post Office. Then I can pay you."

I repeat his words back to him using my own, "I need to go to the post office, buy a telegram, write on it that I QUIT, and mail it to you here?" He nods his head while my blood boils.

"NO! I will NOT do that! This has gone on long enough! I'll just go get my lawyer, see what they have to say." I bluff in the same tone that mamma used.

"No, no, this is law! It has to be this way, I promise!" Andrew leans forward on the bar and uses his eyes to convince me this is real. We have a rapport, and I know him to be a good man. I believe him, which is probably worse, because now I have yet another step between me and my paycheck.

"You can just buy it, have them stamp it, and bring it back here. You don't have to wait for the mail."

"Oh, thank god! I can do that." Anxiety fades into an intense focus on a new mission. Andrew commits to stay at the restaurant until I return. The post office is two kilometers down the pier. I can jog there and be back in thirty minutes.

I arrive at the steps of the Post Office, breathing heavily, but I'm still able to run a few more miles if that lawyer thing catches up to me and I have to evade the police. I greet the postman behind his window and explain my situation.

"Necesito una Telegrama de Renuncia." I don't want one, I don't wish to have one, I *need* this certified resignation letter, and I need it now! Tiny bits of anger and frustration slip through my tone towards this nice postman, but we both recognize it as frustration.

"Calmate, señor. I understand what you need, I just need to see your passport. You have it, yes?"

I've become complacent over the last eight weeks. I feel local, I've been living amongst the people, living life in the city. I haven't needed identification since I got here!

My passport can open many gateways, but I now stand in front of one that leads to my paycheck and I forgot the key. Without my telegram, I will be homeless in Argentina. I do not have the key. When I left Sama's this morning, I was too excited and left my passport behind.

"Mierda! No, no lo tengo!"

The postman explains, like Andrew, that they can do nothing without my identification. I tell him my sad story and I attempt to negotiate, but it is futile. I must go back to Sama's and get my passport.

This is Easter weekend and the post office closes early at 3 pm, two hours from now. I can make this, the bus to Sama's takes 45-minutes. If I'm quick, round trip is 90-minutes, with a smidgen of time to run upstairs at Sama's, or spend a few minutes waiting for a bus.

I first need to go back to Cholilas and to tell Andrew I will be late. I trot down the post office stairs, sliding down the end of the handrail. My gentle jog accelerates into a full speed run.

Halfway to Cholila's, I see the 64A bus a block away. This is mine, I need to catch this now! I cannot waste fifteen minutes until the next one, the post office will not wait for me. If I do not get this done now, I need to wait through a three-day weekend, broke, living with a very angry family. Or living in the park, I'm not sure how this is going to go.

I don't have time to tell Andrew what has happened, I know the postman's schedule, but I'm not sure about Andrew. I can only hope he will still be there with my check if I make it back in two hours.

I jump on the bus and exit at Sama's place, her dad lets me in. "Hola, y que..." I push past him with, focused and determined. I'm sure he knows I'm getting paid today. I pay no attention to papa, but It's ok, we're cool.

I grab my passport from my pack and skip down the stairs to catch the return bus to the post office. Papa pokes his head out of the door and looks down the stairs. I yell up at him, "Hablamos despues! We'll talk later!"

I arrive at the postman's window at 2:50. "Did you get it? Si?" he asks excitedly, like he's rooting for his favorite team. I hand him my passport. He quickly prints out a little receipt, confirmation that I've mailed a telegram to my place of work that says, "I quit."

"Aquí está! Now you can go!" I do.

There is one phrase that I've heard continually throughout this continent. I heard it on New Year's Eve when Jimi's father was lighting fireworks. I heard it in Chiclayo, Peru, when I was expelling from both ends. I hear it again now, inside my head, while Andrew counts out $434 on the bar. *Salir corriendo* - to leave running. That is exactly what I will do, first thing in the morning.

I am no longer a destitute local, my wallet is padded again. My route will turn me back into a foreigner, surpassing the need to settle. I need to travel again. The road has been screaming at me to come back, and with the power of a telegram, I remove homelessness from my near-term prospects. I feel an intense push from Buenos Aires and an even stronger pull towards my beacon. It's time to extend my borders again.

I haven't had this much cash since my first few weeks in Argentina. If I could sense the future when I first got here, or if I had the courage to change my path, I would have turned around and went back to Bolivia. But now I am back at that cross-roads, with a chance to do it all over again. Fate wins.

My adoration of Sama and Argentina has been boiled in a vat of humility, but the bubbles are settling and the fog is diffusing. My options are coming back, but I must be both careful and quick if I want to get home. I have a second lifeline, but it comes with strict conditions, ones I have not yet known on this continent. I must now stay resolute, if I do not, I have no parachute.

This injection of cash gives me a longing for home. I can get there now, my real home, not these temporary make-believe bases. My mind wanders to Washington and then to Alaska. It's been too long, too much, I need to decompress, I need to find my way home, I need to rest from the madness.

I can either travel moderately through Bolivia, or I can shotgun it straight to Lima, and up to the majestic Machu Pichu for my final days. I have the time and money to see one more place before I leave South America, and I've reduced it to either Bolivia or my original beacon.

My reasons for being in Argentina have disappeared, and there is nothing for me in Chile. I call the airport in Lima to set my dates. I have ten days to get to Lima before my plane leaves without me, again. I'll take the 35-hour bus to La Paz, Bolivia, rest for a few days, and then bus straight to Lima to catch my final flight.

Sama and I slowly stuff my pack, often pausing to exchange wry glances. We've only known each other for a few months, but we both feel like we've missed an opportunity. I have lingered here to see if flowers would bloom, but instead, I leave them wilted in the shadows. Sama is my first exploration into the spontaneity of human kind, and my quest to understand roots as balanced against wings. She chooses roots. I choose wings.

I heave my backpack upon my shoulders and wrap my arms around Sama. I give her a sailor's kiss, dipping slightly, until the weight of my pack pulls us both over, bouncing us flat on the bed. We giggle. She cradles my cheek in her hand, as I did on the bus from Salta. I reciprocate and then slowly withdraw from the room.

Week Twenty-Three | *April 11*

The smell of rubber and diesel surround the central bus station in Buenos Aires. A stone statue of a soldier sits atop his horse, pointing the way to the station entrance. Trains and buses both share this station. It is a cross-road, a convergence where the people that are coming can merge with those that are going, regardless of the mode of travel. Unless you're flying, of course.

I plot my escape to Lima through Bolivia, skipping around Chile entirely. I map out the dollars, the roads, the taxis, the buses, the hostels, and the dates. It will absorb all my cash to go this route, but after a week, I will arrive in Lima ready to take my plane home to Seattle.

I know this continent. I am returning to the familiar billow of the winds and the pull of the road. I can finally venture away from the prescribed life of Buenos Aires and that fickle thought that I should settle down.

The direct bus to lima leaves in an hour, but the bus to Bolivia doesn't leave until later tonight. If I go through Bolivia, there will be many obstacles, and if I trip I cannot get another job. I have no more lifelines; the path is narrow. I must finally opt for stability and security. In one hour, I will be on the bus to Lima through Chile.

It will take three days to get to Lima, but then this Argentinian detour will end, my circle complete. I'll be back in my bed on the rooftop of Hostel España, down the dusty street from my favorite corner cantina, with more than a week to wander and contemplate my choices and my new history.

The bus is full, except for one empty seat right next to me. Everyone on board is loaded down, either with children or with bags, many with both. They are moving their families and their homes, while I try to find my way back to my own flag.

I board, throw my daypack in the seat, climb next to the window and listen to the voice in my head scream "Let's go!" I am ready. For thirty more minutes, the women and children struggle to settle down and move in. It's a three-day bus, they can resolve their comfort later! Finally, the bus engine roars in sync with my heartbeat.

As morning breaks, we pass through the shadow of the mighty Mount Aconcagua, the highest mountain in the Americas. As our bus crests the mountain range, I realize that these people will be in my immediate space for the next eighty hours. I am free, I should mingle.

We are energized by the sunrise and the scenery, as morning chatter quickly envelopes the bus. I help a little boy find his toy, smile at his grandma, and force myself to make new friends. Somehow there's always a pretty girl on these trips, and this is no exception.

We stop in Santiago, but I stay close to the bus. I don't trust myself. Many passengers debark, other faces appear, and we depart shortly after sunset. In two days, I'll be back on the trail, immersed in familiar sights. Lima is calling. The beacon is brightening.

After sixteen hours due east, we roar north. The serenade of the smooth pavement sings its lullaby, while we hug the divide between land and water - ocean and continent. The familiar bleak desert parades by the opposite windows, but on my side, I stare out at an endless field of water, the Pacific Ocean. The path will soon go even further north up this coast line, all the way to Alaska, where I can rejoin my own tribe, but first I need to get through this desolate Chilean coastline - again.

We pass towns and beaches that I visited with Sama and Val during our first misadventures. I envision my topless Sama bouncing in the saltwater and the mirages prancing by on the hot beach air, before all hope turned to despair.

It is the same land, the same highway, the same crossing, but I am a different person. I have no pasta in my backpack, no funds for bribes and no dreams of grandeur. There are no severed goat's heads lining the sidewalk sending omens. I ponder if their presence at the beginning and their absence at the end are equally symbolic, highlighting the edges that stretch between these extremes.

The bus rolls northward, past the Nazca lines, which I had hoped to see when I was here the first time. Carved deep into the stones, the lines comprise intricate patterns, some with geometric precision and others etched like a set of children's drawings. Presumably, they were carved into the surface of the earth by extraterrestrials. It's as if an alien father and his alien child were using the desert landscape as a practice canvas, looking down on the surface from their space ships, a father teaching his son how to draw with a huge alien laser pen. Unfortunately, I can see nothing from the bus but barren land.

I ask the driver, "Can I get out here? I'll catch another bus." I have time and cash, I'll be fine.

"I can't stop you from leaving, but I can't open the baggage compartment either. It's sealed for security. You need to pick up your bag in Lima." He shakes his head, bowed low, and gets back on the bus.

I'm close to Lima, it's only another 500 kilometers, but something is telling me not to leave this bus and get dumped in southern Peru without my backpack. I follow the driver up the stairs, slunk back in my chair, and await our arrival to Lima.

We are in the final eight-hour stretch. That's less than a full work day at Cholila's. We'll be in Lima very soon. It's a damn good thing too, I'm getting easily irritated by these same people, this same small space, the vibration of the wheels on the road, and this constant hum in my head. All the little kids are either running around the bus or crying with their mothers.

The third and final night arrives. Our bus navigates the streets of the Peruvian capital, coming to rest at the central station. I have been dependent upon this bus for too long. It is time to say goodbye to my window seat.

While the other families are shuffling around, gathering their baskets, I quickly exit with my daypack and go straight to the luggage compartment. I wait for ten minutes, wondering if I should break the security seal and grab my bag myself. The driver was adamant back in Nazca that the seal shall not be touched, but I really must get out of this station and back to my route.

The Revived Life

21

They still remember me.

I hand Pedro some cash and he hands me my key. I enter the familiar courtyard. I see the steps that go up to my rooftop room, but not as many tables are blocking the pathway. The furniture has thinned, just like the clientele.

No one is perched on the railings that overlook from the second floor. No one is sitting at the tables in the café. There are no new faces here for me to guide through the back alleys of Lima. The energy is different now. It is deserted and the stench of humility permeates the air.

I have overstayed my welcome both in Buenos Aires, and on this entire continent. All places prepare for winter, even if time is inverted and the toilets swirl opposite. The seasons are changing, and the tourists are thinning. I must get home! The honeymoon is over, but I have one more climax before I vacate this continent.

My plane to Seattle left three weeks ago while I was in Argentina, but I have found my way back to my departure point. The airline honors my ticket and confirms the date. In eight days, they'll take me from the south to the north, across the western hemisphere to my home port in Seattle. I have a week for Cusco and to complete a promise that I made to myself six months ago.

When morning breaks, I stroll down the stairs, and look over the handrail with intentions to have a coffee and find transport to Cusco. I sit alone, but I see ten or twelve Israelis checking in at the lobby. I scan the crowd. They are all men, except for one. I lock eyes with a pale, dark-haired, perfectly formed young lady in holey jeans. Her smoky eyes are fixated on me as well. Her gaze entices me to rise from my seat and approach.

Week Twenty-Four | Sunday

It's been three days. I arrived in Lima firmly intent on a direct route to Machu Pichu, but then I met an Israeli beauty. Boarding her ship in the night has hijacked my plans. We are simply two travelers crossing paths and enjoying the pleasures of passing. We all travel to the same places, but on our own schedules. Not all of life's wishes of longevity can come to fruition. I say goodbye.

The bus to Cusco takes 38 hours and costs $40. It's the tail end of the wet season during an El Nino year. The climates merge and create downpours that make the roads impassable. When I was on my route down the Andes a few months ago, I spent nearly thirty hours on various busses, stopped, just waiting for road crews to clear landslides. Aside from the roads giving way, and the Shining Path rebels, any other number of adversities may occur if I continue over land. This reminds me of Bolivia, and other temporary dreams of longevity.

The flight from Lima to Cusco leaves daily and costs $70. An hour flight would seem instant as compared to the buses I've been taking. I can't wait for the bus. I must invest in another flight that will get me there in now. I'm becoming a regular jetsetter. This is my reward for passing the Israeli ship without getting anchored.

I sit in the Lima airport again, just as I did when Sama and Val took me to Chile. This time though, I am alone. My choices, mixed with those from people I've met along the road, have lead me to this bench again, wondering where everyone has gone. I wait for my flight to the Lost City of the Incas, my shining beacon. The majestic Machu Pichu summons me and I will answer.

I board the small twin-propeller plane from the tarmac with about twenty strangers. We lift off and head east towards the mountains. I am reminded of the rugby team that came through here in the 1970's. They crashed into one of these peaks, desperately isolated, hundreds of miles from any civilization. After first surviving the plane crash, then avalanches, thirst and hunger, and then resorting to cannibalism, a few were eventually rescued but lived forever jaded.

I sit on my hands, cross my fingers and ride the turbulence. I look out the window and imagine which peak they crashed on. This can't be healthy for my psyche to imagine my death.

This one-hour flight does *not* turn into months of cannibalism. I can stop imagining how the other passengers would taste. Instead, we land safely at Cusco airport precisely on schedule.

Cusco sits honorably on a plateau atop one of the highest peaks in the range. Perched at 3,500 meters, this is a full kilometer higher than Cajamarca, where I got altitude sickness and liquefied my insides. Can one develop antibodies for altitude sickness? I can't get sick again. The trek on the Inca Trail is three days and I will be miles from anything civil, such as hospitals.

In Cajamarca, the Danes were my caretakers. I could stay in my room to focus on healing and sleeping. They brought comfort through their presence and the assortment of pills they brought back.

In Cusco, I will not have their console. There will be no one here to care for me. It's just me. I need to be careful. I need to spend a few days climatizing before I ascend higher into the clouds toward the ruins.

I first came south through Ecuador, bouncing across the peaks, visiting a few of these top-ten highest cities in the world, but I still got sick when I stopped in Cajamarca. That was four months ago. This time my route is from Argentina which sits comfortably at sea level. Here in Cusco, my bowels are getting nervous. I need to find some coca leaves and an enzyme stone to thin my blood.

Today, I attempted to perpetuate my immortality by drinking from the Incan Fountain of Youth. About twenty minutes outside of Cusco, an aquifer of fresh mountain water flows majestically between man-made stones that have become glued together by time and toil. The wall has a steady stream of water pouring into a trough that drains into the earth. The flow of water never runs dry, alluding to the myth of its eternal properties for anyone who drinks here. May it impart upon me the gift of longevity and further contribute to my cosmic ribbon.

I have five more days until I catch my plane out of Lima on Saturday. That's enough time to drink from the fountain of youth, see the lightening ruins, and then hike to see mother herself. Cusco is ripe with culture and commerce, history and energy, but my resources are thinning for a second time. I've exhausted any avenues of replenishment and all of my lifelines.

The opportunities to linger have faded. One more experience, one more evolution, one more escape before I venture back into reality. My soul has become whole since I was last at home, but I am ready to bask in the comfort of my own kind.

The mountains, the deserts, and the jungles have taken me in. My circle is complete, but first one more. I must immerse and I must explore.

Week Twenty-Four | Monday

Months ago, when I went fishing for piraña with Moipa and the Hourani, I saved the teeth from the piraña I caught. They have been nestled safely in my pack through the length of Ecuador and Peru, across northern Chile, through the gaucho's Argentina into the metropolis of Buenos Aires. They were with me on the route back through Chile and up to Peru, and over to the mountains again. They are with me now, but not for much longer.

These piraña teeth have been my talisman, my only tether tying me to the roots of this winter, going all the way back to Jimi. They are my anchor and my constant. They summon time and keep me ever present to the path in front of me. But this time, the sage comfort they provide will desert me.

The young lady lays her blanket upon the walkway that leads to the church in the central plaza. Her two long braids are shadowed by her woolen shawl, as they hang across her shoulders and into her lap. Her intricate jewelry is laid out on her blanket, first the necklaces and then the rings. She is my age, with caramel skin, a warm smile and peaceful eyes. She is electric but soothing.

I approach, browse her offerings, and play coy. We make small talk, until I reach into my pocket to extract my teeth. "Can you make something with these?"

She studies them, turning them over in her palm and poking them with her forefinger. "Are these piraña teeth?" She asks, I confirm. "I'll make you something muy especial." She is sweet and sincere. "But it will take me a while. You can pay me half now and the other half when I finish. Come back at 9 o'clock?"

"Absolutely." I give her the teeth that I've held so close along with $10. It's early, I have a few hours to walk around the evening streets and explore Cusco's crevices before coming back to collect my masterpiece of teeth.

While waiting for the vendor to finish my necklace, I chat with an English couple who are also meandering the market. "Have you been up to the ruins yet?" I ask. They ask which ones, and I clarify, "the motherlode, Machu Pichu. Have you done the treks?"

The Spanish invaded this area in 1535, establishing Cusco as their seat of power. The surviving Incas fled to Machu Pichu, and the Spanish didn't follow them. They never found Machu Pichu and the Incas never came down. They were cut off from the rest of the world.

Historians claim that some strange illness killed all the Incas, but I prefer to romanticize other ends to this great civilization. Did they board a spaceship and fly away? Did they move their gold north and hide at El Dorado, the lost city? Maybe they're still there. Maybe they were just sick.

After the Spanish invade and the Incas die, mother nature is the next successor to the throne and begins to rule the trails. These peaks see frequent rain, creating rock slides that wipe out the entrance points. The dense growth quickly covers any foot trails. The remaining Incas are facing extinction by disease, they aren't concerned with road maintenance.

265

The earth obscures the massive stone bricks that cross the mountainside, as everything fades into history. Over the next five centuries, isolation and mystery dissolve the Incan lifestyle into legend.

Some say the local Cusco Quechuans have always known about Machu Pichu but kept it a secret from the Spanish invaders. In 1911, Hiram Bingham found a piece of pottery that led him to a stone, which led him to a path, which led him up the hill to one of the greatest archeological discoveries of our time.

In contrast to the three-thousand-year-old ruins of Chavin, Machu Pichu is modern. Machu Pichu was built as a royal estate to the Incan Emperor in the 14th century. It was a religious retreat and a ceremonial center to host the events throughout the Incan calendar.

The compound is arranged in perfect alignment with the mountains to worship the sun and the solstices. At each of the two primary gates, visitors can find a large staging area for their llamas, their supplies, and other goods to trade.

This English couple just got back from the ruins and are a perfect pair to educate me on what comes next. "How adventurous are you?" They ask. I shrug my shoulders and let my ragged appearance speak for me.

"The train goes to the small village of Aguas Calientes at the base of Machu Pichu. Then you can take a bus all the way to the top. The route is four hours, so the train also makes two stops along way. The first is the trailhead for a seven-day hike." I remind myself not to get distracted, I have somewhere to be in five days.

"The second stop is the two-day hike, but if you miss this stop you will have to go to the village and just take a bus to the top."

There is no three-day hike! The universe senses my trepidation towards time, and like a child's spanking, reduces my hike by a day.

There is more to be seen in these mountains than just the beacon, I need the context that surrounds the ruins. What made them come to be? What was the journey like? What did the ancient Incas feel as they traversed the spine of the continent, going to sell their commerce?

The surrounding areas tie the culture together. The land binds the stories of the people who farmed these lands, who lived then died at the Spanish hands. They are masterful architects of stone, blending boulders into walls that have endured centuries. They also sacrificed virgins.

I've been sitting on the steps of the cathedral in the Plaza de Armas, listening to the English couple tell me the history of the area and the routes to take. I wait patiently for the pretty merchant to return with my piraña teeth.

She is two hours late, she's not coming back. Now that I think about it, she was overly excited about my teeth when I showed them to her. What's worse, I gave her $10 in advance, effectively paying her to steal my precious talisman right from under me. I mope back to my room and prepare for my train ride tomorrow morning.

Week Twenty-Four | Wednesday

The 6 am train from Cusco to Aguas Calientes is energetic and alive. There are about fifteen backpackers and a handful of locals, intermingled and talking in gestures and Quechua Spanish. Some Andeans dressed in alpaca shawls and Panama hats come through the train playing pan flutes and selling coca leaves. The energy sends ripples through our spirits and the air vibrates.

I'm traveling with two French guys I met at the pub last night, but we're not attached. Depending on their pace, I might just hike to Machu Pichu by myself. For now, I'll stay with them and see how this goes.

Thirty minutes after we leave Cusco, the train slows down, seemingly in the middle of nowhere. Four travelers disembark. This is the trailhead for the seven-day hike. I momentarily sulk since I can't go, but we wave goodbye as they start their unique week. We roll on.

We gain speed and the rattle of the steel wheels seem to sing Machu Pichu Machu Pichu. We ching-chang on the train tracks for another thirty-minutes and then it begins to slow down again.

We are here. This is the trailhead to the three-day hike. The French guys jump out first. I follow them, and two more pairs of hikers exit behind me. The train jerks again and disappears down the rails, leaving us in a peaceful quietness between the jagged peaks.

We start walking, briefly playing leapfrog on the trail with the others from our train. We race ahead to set our own pace, bouncing down the stone pathways. There is no one around. The world is ours.

The path is steep and winds through the mountain in lockstep with the river below. It's as if one of the gods have taken a mighty sword and slashed it right across the ribs of the ranges, gouging out the Inca Trail from the body of the mountains.

These are the original paths that the Andeans took. Along these cobblestone terraces, we pass the remnants of worn farm houses, cut from granite. They stand bravely over the valley, standing strong against the world, but they now are deserted and bested by time.

We hike along the sides of the massive peaks. The Urubamba River is just a sliver far below, like a snake slithering through the bends and folds. If I get lost, I'll just go down to the river and float back to Cuzco.

We rest at the Wiñay Wayna ruins. We sit perched on a ridge that has forever stared towards the valley floor. If I were ever to slip and fall to my death, this is where I would want it to happen, in the crisp air surrounded by this beauty.

We leave Wiñay Wayna and hike to the outpost near the ruins. We see a shack ahead, this is where we will sleep tonight. We enter, and see familiar faces from the train, plus another handful of hikers that left many days ago and just completed the seven-day hike.

We share our stories of the Andes and beyond, imagining how it would have been to live like an Incan. We roll out our bags on the wooden floor, turn out the lights, and wiggle around until we drift to sleep.

At 4 am, Pepe taps me on the shoulder and asks in his French accent if I want to go to the back door. Slightly confused in this early hour, I start to question his relationship with his buddy and if I'm a third wheel in this relationship. "Back door?" I ask.

Pepe reminds me about the Sun Gate. It leads to Machu Pichu from south of the citadel, from behind the city - the back door.

These early morning hours are the most mystical time to see the ruins, we can't be late. We slide on our pants, pack our gear and head out the door. The other travelers are still rumbling in their sleeping bags. I appreciate the speed of these Francs. I can't sleep anyway.

Our headlights illuminate our paths.

I follow in Pepe's steps like I was taught when I climbed Cotopaxi. A short 90 minutes later, we stop and shine our flashlights on two ten-foot-tall pillars. They have faded from the years. We pan the area with our headlights. The pillars stretch into ledges, then walls with small windows.

This must be The Sun Gate! It is still pitch black and we are here already. This explains why everyone else was still back at the cabin sleeping. We park our bags in darkness and examine the outpost. We sit. We wait. We wonder if this is really the Sun Gate. I see no sun.

After an hour, we hear a noise in the trail behind us, and the rest of our cabin mates arrive. It is still black, but we make new friends and laugh at our punctuality. The sun starts to break into dawn and melt the shroud of clouds into the misty valley below. We can now see our surroundings in the surrealistic hue of dawn, but the mighty ruins are still cloaked in fog.

The fog hangs over the ruins like a halo, slowly rising to become enlightened, revealing a history once concealed. The warmth of dawn further burns the cloud cover away. The curtains retract, unveiling the lost city of the Incas.

Three llamas dot the walkway down to the main courtyard, where two more llamas finish their grass breakfasts. The stone foundations remain unshaken despite centuries of wear and neglect. The paths are like old man hands, wrinkled by effort and time.

I close my eyes and listen to the wind. I imagine how many days an Andean would have traveled to arrive at this exact Sun Gate. I imagine how this place would feel with thatched rooves intact and vibrant pan-flutes carrying the tunes on gentle winds.

The tribes of farmers and believers, living pure, pass each other with their llama traffic and selling their goods. On these lands, a different kind of human thrived. One at peace and absent of modern constructs. But then again, when I get to the site I'm going to lay down on their alter of human sacrifice just because I can. I guess no society is perfect.

The path carves its way downward, around the mountain's ridges, weaving its way toward the entrance. I hop and skip down the well-trodden trail, arms swinging wildly, slowing down only to offer admiration and respect to the wild llamas.

The mossy pathway opens to a field where children must have played games. A stone wall appears, and then another field. More stone structures line the edges of the grass. Maybe these were homes, or maybe stables, or maybe something more sinister - maybe a dungeon. We are our own guides on this adventure.

The dim fog has turned into low cloud cover, as the sun peeks its nose under the sheets. My legs wander the site, while my imagination runs wild through time, reconciling my own peace. I lay at the altar of sacrifice.

Shortly after we entered the complex, everyone dispersed around the ruins to find their own centers. Hours later, we hear a faint rumble from far below, near the distant river at the base of the mountain. The sound pulls us from our respective corners of Machu Pichu and we all converge in the main field. We have bonded through hours of peaceful meditation atop these mighty ruins, just us and the land, reigning in serenity.

The rumble slowly ascends. It takes us a moment, but we soon realize that the tourist buses are making their way up the mountain, weaving through the switchbacks. They get closer, and we chatter in finality, reveling in our last few minutes of whimsical connections to this place. We are about to be overrun by the masses.

The busses come to a hydraulic stop on an open field east of the ruins. We walk out and greet them. We have become the stewards of Machu Pichu. She has been ours exclusively for hours, but we are not her only children. She welcomes everyone. She is delighted to be out from the shade of the clouds and no longer lost to the world for centuries.

Me to We

22

The course has corrected itself and now points north. The peripheral view of my past overpowers the need to stay in one place for too long, the pull of the future drives me. Eventually the cosmic ribbon recedes and lies dormant until it is awoken again by soft winds.

The battles we fight within ourselves reveal the things we appreciate, for without them we are lost and without purpose. I have learned much, but I still let the universe carry me on its back. I just float along, connected to the ribbon to see where it floats next. Thankfully, it usually just takes me home.

I am back in Walla Walla now. My soul flows full from the wild ride that just ended. Next year may be even stranger depending on where I land. I want to put my ear to the well and listen to the stories that the world tells.

Year Five | *The Triangle*

I must find Rob! He's a long-time constant, a root to the crew. He is pivotal. Rob is a skinny pale guy, jeans and t-shirts, who seems ready to scrap with anyone on a moment's notice. His feisty persona usually takes him out of town, away from people, into the forests that surround Walla Walla. He camps, hunts, and builds fires. He also smokes a bale of weed daily. He's pure and means no one any harm, but he is guarded.

"I'll get my shit ready, just come pick me up when you get back!" When I left for Quito, Rob said he wanted to go back to Alaska with me. At the time, I was impartial, but I welcome him to align his trajectory with mine.

I'm home now, but it's almost May and I'm a month late! Like Jazmin coming to Costa Rica, or Colin coming to Alaska, worlds will merge again if Rob from the core crew joins with my winter friends in Valdez.

The first trip to Alaska with Ethan and Amber was poorly coordinated and I was left deserted. The second trip with Colin was awkward. It ruined a friendship, but most likely it was just bad chemistry.

It with be different with Rob. He is looking for a lifestyle not a party. I believe him, he is genuine, but he still has an unrepentant angst. I want to be sure of what lies beneath his intentions before we embark.

Now that I've been to Alaska a few times, in addition to whatever just happened in South America, I have learned to pick better travel partners. The road has educated me. Rob is also very wise, he has navigated many crossroads of his own, he'll do well.

I clarify for him, "I don't' live comfortably by most standards. It's a primitive lifestyle." Although we are like brothers, I interrogate Rob to ensure his motivation is proper motivation for this drastic change, one which will also impact my own experience. This is a job interview to be my sidekick.

I turn and look at Rob. "I don't have a place to stay, other than a rusty van at the harbor, but you can camp at Hippy Hill a short walk away. After we set up camp, we'll figure out the rest." I paint a scary picture to prepare him. We may end up homeless in the winter or eaten by bears.

Rob nods vigorously "Grasshopper! I know! That's exactly why I want to go! You know I spend most of my time in the mountains, it's where I live, it's where I breathe. It's where I want to be. Can you help me?"

I know his world, it was my world before I joined the Marines. Rob has stayed in Walla Walla for too long and everything evolved around him. He's stuck and stagnant, looking for a way out. Come with me, Rob, I know the escape route.

"I'm home now, but the last six months in South America have engraved my path." I tell Rob about Ecuador and what Moipa taught us in the jungle. I tell him about longevity, and the lessons that San Pedro teaches, and about our connections to the earth and the ribbon.

"In Lima, time slowed down. I looked around and put my pack on the ground. When Sama said "Atacama!" the wind turned easterly and blew us through the desert!

We were citizens of nowhere, between the borders of countries where life doesn't live."

I integrated through work, family, and play, but Sama's just one of those dames that gets away. Barely making my own escape, I found the route to the lighthouse and to my bright shining beacon.

I turn to Rob and offer a relieved "...but I am home now and I want to go somewhere new again." I see my future clearly, but I am unsure how far Rob wants to take this journey. "I have a mission, though. No matter what happens throughout the summer, I'm saving enough money to go do something. I intend to work very hard so that I can disappear into the world again. You game?"

"Where are you going?" Rob asks.

"I can't answer that yet, I just got back!" I'm excited to be home, but my eyes are open to new possibilities now. I know how to see the world and live throughout it. I've stumbled upon a little secret, and I want to share it. Sama was supposed to be coming, but in her absence, I will need to find another partner.

"I might go see some of the people I just met in South America or follow through on some of the extreme ideas I learned about while I was there.

Paul from England said wants to take the Trans-Siberian railroad from Moscow, across the top of Russia, all the way to Tokyo. I didn't even know that was a thing!

Dara wants to meet up in India next year, but it's not a Kumbha Mela year. I wouldn't be able to see the big Sadhu festival, maybe I'll wait two years to go see India, that festival sounds unique.

"Fran is in Australia and she said I can stay with her in Sydney. Australia has always held many mysteries for me, with her deserts, her reefs and the kangaroos."

Fran was nice, but right now that sounds a little like the time I fell in love, moved to Buenos Aires, spent all my money and nearly became homeless. Following Fran to Sydney seems odd for our platonic relationship.

Manya said I can come to Amsterdam and share her apartment down by the canals, but I'm not sure if I want something as modern as Europe for my next trip. I seek the exotic. I lie. It's just too expensive there.

Maybe I'll start in Turkey and go through Israel and walk the paths of Christ. I can stop in Tel Aviv, then spend a while in Jerusalem, Damascus, and Petra. The Giza pyramids can act as my new beacon. I need to research that option thoroughly before I commit. There is turmoil in that region.

I might go into Africa, but I didn't really hear any stories about this continent. It's always called to me, but I've learned there are other places I need to see first.

I stop to gather my thoughts, tilt my head back, and envision the globe. "These places all offer significantly different experiences than I just lived for the last seven months. I'm home now, and I need to get reacquainted with my old self before I decide what to do next."

Rob lights another bowl, while I continue.

"I may also spend some time in Asia somewhere along the timeline. There's a route from Beijing to Bali that looks refreshing." I stop talking and look at Rob. He is sitting more still that I've ever seen him. His head is cradled by his hoodie, as he leans back against the couch.

"These are the things I want to do. These are the destinations I want to know. Does this interest you?" I offer Rob a shortcut past the last few crazy years I spent looking for this lifestyle loophole. He won't need to fumble around in the dark, I can show him the footsteps, but he'll need to keep up or settle down somewhere along the way.

"But Rob, you will need to work crazy hard this summer." The vibrato in my voice and my intense Marine Corps stare wreaks of assurance. He is intent on my words. He is looking for the lifestyle, not the party.

"Dude, I know what it is. I can create my own way." Rob has grown frustrated with my probing, but any trepidation is masked by his eagerness. I know this energy that Rob has, it runs deep in my veins too. It is the same energy that Ethan and Amber shared when talking about going to Kenai, extending me a ladder to climb out of my hole. It's the same anxiety I felt at every border crossing. Rob needs a fresh start and I know how to get him there. I welcome him to join me on this journey.

The mood turns from interrogation to acceptance. I embrace Rob and tell him more about my past summers. "I worked the boats and the canneries, but I'm telling ya Rob, we can skip that and just work in the kitchens. The pay is similar, the work is consistent, the lifestyle is better, and you smell like steak instead of fish slime!" This will be epic, I'm glad he confirmed his reasons and put my anxiety to rest. I'm just getting back on my feet and I don't want to stumble again. I'm very clumsy.

Rob straightens up and recoils backward, his wingspan consuming the couch. "I tried to get Gavin to come too, but he was slow to collect cash. It slips through his fingers like desert sand," Rob says, keeping with the theme of my Atacama exploits. "He really wants to come, but not this year." That would have been cool, but Rob will be a solid travel partner and a new experience unto itself.

"When are we leaving?" Rob asks.
"Let's check on tickets. You ready anytime?"
"Yes, let's go, I'm ready now! You were late!"

When I left Machu Pichu, I flew back to Lima, stayed one night and flew straight to Seattle. I took the bus to Spokane for a quick visit and then stopped to fully decompress in Walla Walla a week ago.

The compass and clock will now run in reverse, as I go back through the triangle on the way back north. I've stopped in my hometown and picked up a partner. It is a new year and a new cycle, but this is becoming constant.

In seven days, we will fly out of Seattle and into Anchorage. Our week is mapped, and we say our goodbyes to Walla Walla and our hometown. I haven't been here long enough to get reattached to my old nefarious ways or the people that prescribe them, but Rob has known little else. When leaving a home base, there is a heavy weight on one's core. I sympathize with Rob, but he is ready.

We stop in Spokane on our return route through the triangle. I think we made Gavin feel bad that he's not coming with us. He still hosts us for four days, sharing his couch, his liquor, and his time. Of course, the lights always come on and the party always ends. It's time to take our bus to Seattle, and then fly to Alaska.

We sit hypnotized by the roaring wheels on the highway that last long into the evening hours. In Seattle, we transfer and take a shuttle to the airport.

We wander like lost boys for hours, anxiety boiling over like lightning bolts from fingertips, until we finally board our flight at midnight.

We land in Anchorage at 4 am. It is dark and chilly, winter is trying to weep away into summer, but there are still more tears to be cried. I'm here about a month later than the last few times I came, so it's warmer, but it's still a few weeks early and the chill remains.

"What now?"

"Now we wait." I drop my pack next to a bench and sit down on the floor next to it. The Anchorage airport is silent except for a vacuum cleaner at the next gate.

"This is what happens when we take the cheap red-eye flight!" It's too early to start hitching, and there's no bus to take us to the highway until 8am. We can't hitch through the city, and a taxi would be a hundred bucks. "Patience, grasshopper," I retort.

After four hours of battling Rob's nervous energy, the Borealis Shuttle Company opens its counter window. "Go talk to the driver, I'm new." We take our packs and climb aboard the shuttle.

"Where am I taking you?" I considered telling him that our ultimate destination is Valdez. Maybe he would drive us all the way there, but I didn't water that thought and it quickly died. I resign to futility and decide we'll stick with the plan.

"Centennial Park, please."

"Park's closed this time of year."

"It isn't the park that we're interested in, just that it is close to the highway. We're hitching to Valdez, and we can't start here." I end up telling him anyway.

"Well, you need to go to Eagle River first, and I can't take you there, I'm just a shuttle. You need to take a bus." He points through the door, towards an empty bench. "That one will take you there, and then you can find your own route."

"Yep, that sounds right!" We exit the shuttle and cross the street to what looks like a bus stop. My eyes follow the shuttle as it drives away. A faded schedule comes into view, stapled to the telephone pole next to the bench. I examine it.

The shuttle driver didn't tell us we would have to wait two more hours for the bus! This feels like the Atacama that I just left, stuck without a ride for hours. But at least here, I'm certain the bus driver will not make innuendos and put his hand on Rob's leg. He's not as pretty as Sama.

"Rob, we wait again," I say towards the ground.

In Ecuador, I spent five hours pushing a canoe through the jungle with a stick waiting for a motor. In Peru, I spent a full day waiting for a crew to clear a rockslide. In Chile, we couldn't get across the desert, and in Argentina I had to wait to get paid. I'm used to waiting, but Rob can't sit still.

"It would have been better if the bus just took us to the edge of town as we planned." Rob's right. We could have done this differently. By the time the bus gets here, we will have been in Alaska for six hours and not moved. This bus only takes us to Eagle River anyway. That's just an hour up the road.

In South America, there were many obstacles that changed my routes, but they all stemmed from my own choices. This time, it's like the holy ghost grabbed us by the scruff, pulled us out of the bus and sat us on this bench. "Sit!" We are now left to ponder our decisions, both past and future, until the bus arrives in the present.

The sun starts to rise at 10 am and brings the bus with it. We hop aboard and watch the green scenery pass. After an hour, the driver stops, and we exit to the side of the road. "You boys gonna be ok?"

We reply affirmatively and in stereo, "Oh yeah."

Rob has his camping gear, I won't need to worry about him. I don't have my gear this time, I eventually sold it in Buenos Aires, but I should still have a van in the middle of a field. This gives me a destination.

My shoes are trashed from the Inca Trail, but they may last through one more summer. I am lugging my haggard backpack, it has become a part of me, it's frame molded to fit my form.

From Eagle River, we hitchhike for a few hours to Palmer. Amber lives here, but we haven't spoken for three years. Our roads have diverged. She also has no idea I am even in the state, but my telepathy is at an all-time high. I'm sure she already knows.

The last time I saw of Amber was when her tail lights were heading back to Anchorage, forcing me to find my way to Ed and Jaybird. Now, the grand path has dropped me off on her doorstep. She may be two blocks from me, she might be on the other side of town, or she might not even be in this state at all.

I make a phone call to the only number I have for her. The phone rings. It rings again. It keeps ringing, with no response by either machine or human. I look at Rob with a stone-cold face.

"That was silly." There's no good reason for us to be in Palmer. We start walking. A truck stops, and we throw our packs in the back and climb inside the canopy.

We cross the snow-covered Thompson Pass and roll into town at 8:30pm. Our chauffeur drives us to the post office, opens the back and lets us out. He then disappears into obscurity like they all tend to do.

The town is dark, but the street lights illuminate the sidewalks, and shed light across the white snow banks. I enter the post office to collect the contents of my box. I have a handful of postcards from my South American friends. I sit on the floor to read a few, but Rob pulls at my jacket, prompting me to show him where he will be sleeping tonight.

Rob and I have the same roots, but we are coming from different directions. Rob has been idle all winter, with his mind intent on moving to Alaska. I've been on vacation for the last six months, accustomed to a slow pace, bound by moments of chaos, but now we sit together surrounded by the serenity of the forests.

We walk across the field. My van is right where I left it. I slide open the side door and it lets out a thunderous roar in the cold, still air. It slams to a stop as it smacks against the hinges. I throw my pack inside.

"Let's get the tent up," Rob says. He aggressively unstraps his tent and tears it from his pack. In record time, it is fully erect like a side-car to my van. Rob grabs his stuff and quickly disappears inside without a word.

"Sleep well, see you in the morning!" I shout to Rob, with cynical overtones, surprised he is retiring. He emerges back from his tent. He gives me a big bear hug and a sly smile. Rob's just tired. I need to remind myself we are coming together through different paces.

"Mañana!" Rob replies, as he crawls back into his tent. I climb inside my van and leave the door cracked open a little. My sleeping bag and pillow is undisturbed, rolled up and sitting against the wall where I left them. I unroll my bag and discover that the winter cold has meticulously preserved it. My bag even retains my smell, although that could be anything these days.

I stashed some propane tanks under the floor panel last summer for my heat and my light. I screw in the heater first and it lights after a few flicks of my flame. My lantern, however, fails to ignite. I'll need to get new wicks tomorrow. I light a cigarette and bask in the warm glow of glorious heat from propane in a confined space.

It takes a few days, but Rob and I connect with Big Al at Oscar's on the Waterfront. I introduce them and they form an instant bond. Rob quickly secures his position on

Oscar's roster as the lead breakfast cook. I'm cooking breakfasts at the Glacier while Rob runs Oscar's in the morning. Then after lunch, I take over for Rob at Oscars and cook dinner. Rob doesn't need two jobs, Rob needs to explore this new environment and integrate. Thus, it is written and so goes our summer.

Rob embraces Valdez and her culture. He moves into a thirty-foot trailer and starts living the high-life. I know where this path goes, it's what I tried to do before I ended up homeless for the winter. Luxury in isolation is the bait, but I'm not a mouse anymore. I won't be trapped.

My friends become Rob's friends, and my Valdez family increases by one significant number. Rob's first immersion is complete, although he has no desire to hang out with my Pentecostal friends and get dipped in the lake. He did that once before, similar at least, and it didn't stick. I also followed that path to its natural conclusion, but for me, it ended at a different destination than Rob.

The Apostolic Pentecostals promised me that god would give me a gift, neatly wrapped and drifting down from the heavens. Instead, he connected me to the earth and showed me how to navigate.

Rob understands the drive to explore, but his thresholds are different. Valdez is his happy place. He doesn't need to look any further.

The summer light has dimmed, and I sever my ties to the Alaskan season. The world is calling. It's been five months and the days are getting shorter. The breath of the city is exhaling, and the people are mostly gone.

Some have returned to college and others left for their southern homes. The fish are gone too, and with them the fishermen. Their influences have all added to my collection of filters through which I see the world.

I'm not sure where I'm going, but I know I will never have been there before. The people - I will know them. Although the faces may change, we are all familiar. We bond through immersions into cultures, stretching the limits of our mortalities. We breathe with the seasons, in sync with the earth.

The energies surrounding this small fishing town are strong, they always pull me into the summer. But now those energies are fading into winter hibernation. I know this sleep. It is hypnotic. The dark times outweigh the bright ones when the gods turn out the sun.

I remind Rob what I told him before we left Walla Walla, "When it's summertime in the north, I'll be here! But when the snow comes and drowns the town in darkness, I can't stay."

Despite my strongest dissuasions, Rob will stay in Valdez through the winter. I'm not sure Rob understands Alaska yet, but neither did I when I first found it. He has made a home here and he fits well. When I get back next spring, Rob will either be vibrant, depressed, or frozen. I will learn which soon enough. We say good bye.

All things mutate, like this moment now or that moment then. The experiences grow and fade, always morphing into the next, until we have a collection called life. Monuments and memories become engrained, yet always dwindle as the moments continue to pass. The seed to the next tree is planted. The cosmos has made its move and the next move is mine.

Traffic is thin since most of the visitors are gone. I don't need to stick out my thumb, it's obvious why I'm here. I sit on my pack, underneath the town's only street light. I've rested long enough, working long days to find a way to get away. It's time to leave, to live, to love, to learn, and to whisper into the winds that blow my way.

Three eagles float overhead, drifting gracefully on the breeze. Behind them, ten crows approach, cackling with sinister intentions. They dive and chase the eagles away, reclaiming the skies for themselves.

The light turns red and a van stops in front of me. The light turns green, but they sit still. I know what comes next. The door slides open and a man waves me closer. Goodbye summer, goodbye Rob, goodbye Valdez. I will see you again when the sun comes back around.

"Where you headed?"
"Anchorage please. Same as you, I presume?"

I hop on a cloud and ride it across the mountains, away from the winter wind blowing at my back. I relinquish my past and compound my identity, with renewed clarity, and float into the beautiful unknown.

Ciao for now…

Proof

Made in the USA
Columbia, SC
10 August 2018